The Bagel Bib

"You won't find a more enthusiastic celebration of bagel noshing."
— *Kankakee (IL) Journal*

"A comprehensive guide to one of Earth's greatest breads . . . lip-smacking, whimsical and fun."
— *Copley News Service*

"What is remarkable about this book is that its [author shares her] knowledge about bagels on a universal scale and that [she knows] how to inject humor into the seriousness of food."
— *Jewish News*, Southfield, Mich.

"If you're seriously looking to improve your bagels, I'd suggest . . . *The Bagel Bible.*"
— *Portland Oregonian*

"Offers pages of suggestions for low fat feasts, breakfast, lunch and dinner, parties and special kids' fare."
— *Indianapolis News*

"It's edible theater in the round. The cookbook and a bag of fresh bagels make an irresistible gift."
— *St. Paul Pioneer Press*

"A fantastic collection of recipes."
— *Fort Wayne (IN) News-Sentinel*

The Bagel Bible

FOR BAGEL LOVERS

The Complete Guide

TO GREAT NOSHING

Second Edition

by

MARILYN BAGEL

assisted by Bette Flax, nutritionist and behavior-modification counselor

The Globe Pequot Press

OLD SAYBROOK, CONNECTICUT

Library of Congress Cataloging-in-Publication Data
Bagel, Marilyn.
        The bagel bible : for bagel lovers, the complete guide to great
        noshing / by Marilyn Bagel ; assisted by Betty Flax. — 2nd ed.
            p.   cm.
        ISBN 1-56440-725-X
        1. Bagels. 2. Cookery (Bagels) I. Title.
    TX770.B35B33   1995
    641.8'15—dc20   95-15386
                                                          CIP

Book design by Nancy Freeborn
Illustrations by Lana Mullen / Mullen & Katz

Manufactured in the United States of America
Second Edition/First Printing

To bagel lovers everywhere, especially those closest to me:

Tom, who made me a Bagel in the first place;

my singing bagel-maker, Florrie; Alan and Amy Abrams;

Evy and Aaron Modance; Alice Bagel;

Jo-Anne and Marty Modance; and Resa Levy.

Contents

Preface

First of all, my last name really is "Bagel." I can appreciate your skepticism. If I met a writer whose last name was Pizza, and she authored a pizza book, I'd roll my eyes, too. Now, on to bagels with a small "b."

These "golden rings" are being discovered by people the world over, and they're producing a culinary and business "gold rush" that's rising faster than yeast. Why now? We're a more nutritionally aware society. Bagels are an excellent source of complex carbohydrates. You feel good when you're eating them (they're chewy and orally gratifying), and they're good for you. People on the run (*aren't we all?*) find bagels easy to take along, whether they're breakfasting in the car, lunching in the office, or carpooling a group of hungry youngsters. Joggers, cyclists, and other fitness enthusiasts love bagels for their energy value. The bulges in those fanny packs are probably bagels!

Just like bagels, my book has something for everyone. As you see by my recipes, bagels are not just for breakfast anymore. You can also make quick and easy lunches, dinners, vegetarian delights, party foods, desserts, and children's favorites.

Bagels are an emotional food that evokes strong feelings. Just read what the dozens of celebrities I surveyed—from Bob Hope, Larry King, Whoopi Goldberg, and Leo Buscaglia to Alan Dershowitz, Sally Jessy Raphael, Jane Alexander, Joan Rivers, Hal David, and Dick Clark—reveal about their bagels.

If you want to bake homemade bagels from scratch in your own kitchen, there's a chapter for you, too. Try my Sesame Whole-Wheat Bagels, Vegetable Garden Bagels, Cheese Duo Bagels, Strawberry Pink Valentine Bagels, and more.

Whether you buy bagels or make them, eating them is what counts. Happy bageling!

Acknowledgments

To Dad for your many hours of help.

My appreciation and a whole-wheat bagel to my nutritionist, Bette Flax, and to Elyse Schneiderman, Ph.D., for steering me in the right direction.

A tip of the Bagel to the hundreds of bagel manufacturers and bagel-bakery owners, large and small, and to the American Institute of Baking and numerous bakery trade publications for their assistance—especially *Baking Buyer, Bakery Production and Marketing,* and *Milling & Baking News.*

Special thanks to Metropolitan Toronto Councillor Norman Gardner.

To Leslie Sides for your rescue oven. And to Judy, Steve, Meredith, and Lizzie Carver for your tastebuds.

To the many readers of my book's first edition for your kind letters.

And, of course, to my friends at the Globe Pequot Press who continue to keep this Bagel on a roll.

Why does a seagull fly over the sea?
Because if it flew over the bay, it would be called a bagel.

When made with kosher products, the recipes in this book are considered to be kosher.

CHAPTER 1

Whatsa Bagel?

Famous Historical Quote:

When told that her country's people had no bread, Marie Antoinette replied, "Let them eat bagels."

Bagels *should* be found in the dictionary under *fun,* but according to Webster (who probably liked his with a *shmear*) a bagel is "a hard bread roll made of yeast dough twisted into a small doughnutlike shape, cooked in simmering water, then baked." The bagel is the only bread product that is boiled before it is baked. That's what gives the bagel its unique texture and the crust its characteristic shine.

Legend has it that in 1683 in Vienna, Austria, a local Jewish baker wanted to thank the king of Poland for protecting his countrymen from Turkish invaders. He made a special hard roll in the shape of a riding stirrup—*Bügel* in German—commemorating the king's favorite pastime and giving the bagel its distinctive shape.

As bagels gained popularity in Poland, they were officially sanctioned as gifts for women in childbirth and mentioned in community registers. Mothers used them as nutritious teething rings that their infants could easily grasp—a practice still popular today.

Bagels eventually made their way to Russia, where they were called *bubliki* and were sold on strings. Like other ring-shaped objects, they were said to bring good luck and possess magical powers. It is even said that songs were sung about bagels!

A North American Debut

When the Eastern European Jewish immigrants arrived in North America at the turn of the century, they brought the bagel with them. Many settled in Canada, giving cities like Toronto and Montreal their reputation for having superb bagels. The American bagel industry established formal roots in New York between 1910 and 1915 with the formation of Bagel Bakers Local #338. This exclusive group of 300 craftsmen with "bagels in their blood" limited its membership to sons of members. At the time, it was probably easier to get into medical school than to get an apprenticeship in one of the thirty-six union bagel shops in New York City and New Jersey.

Professional bagel baking required know-how and backbreaking labor. Bagel makers' sons apprenticed for months to learn the trade. Men were paid by the piece and usually worked in teams of four. Two made the bagels, one baked, and a "kettleman" was in charge of boiling the bagels. The men earned about 19 cents a box, and each box typically contained sixty-four bagels. It was not unusual for a team to make one hundred boxes a night.

With the rising of the yeast in countless bakeries, the popularity of the bagel rose far beyond the boundaries of ethnic neighborhoods. In the late 1950s and 1960s, bakers from New York and New Jersey began moving to other parts of the country. One such veteran who opened a bagel bakery in a suburb of Washington, D.C., in 1966, remembers his skeptical landlord nervously questioning, "Who's gonna spend seven cents for one of *those* things?"

Prepackaged bagels first became available in grocery stores in the 1950s. With the introduction of frozen bagels in the 1960s, consumers had access to bagels even if they didn't live near a bagel bakery.

Bagel-making machines, a boon to commercial bakers, were also introduced in the early 1960s. The machines form bagels by extruding the dough through a ring shape. Inventor Dan Thompson says, "I was born to invent a bagel machine. My father was thinking about a bagel-making machine when I was conceived." That may not be far from the truth, because Dan's father had a wholesale bakery in Winnipeg, Canada, and was already working on a bagel-making machine back in 1926. But it was far too complicated, too slow, and too costly to manufacture and wasn't commercially feasible.

There were as many as fifty unsuccessful attempts to produce a bagel-making machine in the early twentieth century. The Thompson Bagel Machine Corporation developed the first viable model, despite "doubting Thompsons" who insisted that no machine would ever replace the human hand in forming bagels. Most of the early machines were leased by bakers who paid by the dozen on a running timemeter. Now most are purchased. Popular with "Mom and Pop" bagel bakeries is the single-bank Thompson model with dough divider that forms 175 dozen (2,100) bagels an hour. Large-scale production companies use multiples of the double-bank machine, each of which produces 400 dozen (4,800) bagels hourly.

The Low-fat, No-cholesterol Wonder

Bagels are a dream come true if you're watching your weight, your cholesterol, or your fat intake. You'll find bagels on the recommended list of every major diet plan. They have no cholesterol and very little fat. They are highly satisfying, and their chewiness makes them much more emotionally gratifying than a slice of bread. Take a fresh bagel along for a filling low-fat snack, particularly if you plan to be someplace—such as on an airplane—where your food choices will be limited.

Bagels vary in size from baker to baker and manufacturer to manufacturer. They can range from 1-ounce bagelettes (miniature bagels) and 2- to 2.5-ounce sizes that equate to two slices of bread to mega-bagels that tip the scales at 7 ounces or more. On the average, you can figure on the following nutritional content for a 2.5-ounce plain bagel:

37	grams carbohydrate	0	milligrams cholesterol
8	grams protein	390	milligrams sodium
1	gram fat	190	calories

Hot news for good nutrition

Bagels Are Big Business

Bagels have moved from the breadbox to the boardroom. An ever-increasing number of major corporations are in the bagel business at the retail, wholesale, and frozen "bake-off" levels; others manufacture bagel chips and related products.

Among the many companies in the bagel ring are Brueggers Corp., Continental Baking Co. (Hostess Bagels, Katz's Bagel Co.), Corporate Foods Limited of Toronto (Brooklyn Bagel Boys), CPC International (Thomas' Bagels), Castle Baking Co., Interstate Baking Co., King David's bagel chips, Kraft Foods (Lender's Bagels), Manhattan Bagel, Manischewitz, New York Style bagel chips, Pepperidge Farm, The Quaker Oats Co. (Petrofsky's Bagels, Arnie's Bagelicious Bagels, Proof & Bake Frozen Products), Sara Lee, Skolniks, Specialty Foods Corp. (Burns & Ricker bagel chips), Starbucks Coffee Co. (Noah's New York Bagels), Uncle B's, and Western Bagel.

Bagel news gets more ink than ever before in major newspapers from *The New York Times* and *Wall Street Journal* to the *Los Angeles Times.* The bakery industry's darling of the decade, bagels are featured prominently in trade publications including *Bakery Production and Marketing, Baking Buyer, Frozen Food Age, Milling & Baking News,* and *Modern Baking.*

In recent years consumer demand for bagels and bagel products has absolutely exploded, with U.S. sales likely to surpass $1 billion a year. Now considered no more "ethnic" than pizza or tacos, bagels are everywhere—on land, at sea, and in the air—from fast food restaurants to United States Navy ships and commercial airlines. Just who's eating them? Bagel-lovers of every race, creed, color, and religion.

You can find bagels at your local supermarket—at the bakery counter, bread section, deli counter, special self-serve bins, freezer section—and at bagel bakeries, convenience stores, department stores, gas station food marts, even doughnut shops. Some bagel bakeries are open twenty-four hours a day to satisfy the needs of true bagelholics. Los Angeles has originated drive-through bagel bakeries. All this is a far cry from the modest bagel pushcarts on cobblestone streets at the turn of the century. On today's city sidewalks, bagels are sold from high-tech mobile fold-out cappuccino bars.

As bagels continue to become even more popular, this Bagel predicts a host of new products in supermarkets. Soon there may be bagel "holes" stuffed with flavorful fillings, chocolate-covered bagel chips, bagel burgers (a takeoff on popular "bagel dogs"), and bagel French toast. In fact, you'll find the recipes for the last three in this book.

Commercial bagel bakers are responding to this bagel love affair not only by extending their product lines but by refining production techniques. Many are substituting steaming, done with high-tech equipment, for boiling the bagels prior to baking. It speeds production and results in a softer bagel that lends itself more readily to sandwich making: The fillings won't squeeze out when you bite into the sandwich. Diehards argue, however, that it's not a bagel unless the filling "squishes" out when you bite into it!

How the Pros Do It

Bagel bakery owners are fiercely protective of their recipes, guarding them as they would precious jewels. In fact, they keep their recipes in safes.

Professional bagel baking is a tricky process. Many factors significantly affect the outcome: the quality of high-gluten flour (commercial bakers use varieties not available in supermarkets—and experienced bakers can tell by the taste which brand of flour their competitors use and even when and if they switch brands); the water quality (many bakeries install water purification systems); the correct quantities of yeast and salt (too much salt adversely affects the dough's ability to rise); the expertise of the dough maker; the equipment; the mixing time; the use of boiling or steam proof methods; and so on. Even the weather is a factor. As one bagel pro puts it, "Bagel dough is like a human being—it senses temperature." When the weather is warm, bakers use less yeast. In humid or dry conditions, they make other adjustments.

In a professional bagel bakery, after the bagels are formed and have risen, they're placed in a refrigeration unit known as a *retarder*. With a lower humidity than a standard refrigerator, this unit retards the rising process and affects the formation of the crust. The preparation stage called *kettling*—boiling the bagels—gelatinizes the starch that helps form the bagel "skin" and gives bagels their special shine.

In some bagel bakeries, the first stage of bagel baking takes place on burlap-covered redwood boards. The burlap boards are wet down with water; the bagels are then placed on the boards and put in the oven. Among bagel bakers, the expression "flipping the boards" describes the step of turning the bagels over from burlap boards onto the oven hearth.

Perhaps your neighborhood bagel bakers can take a moment when they're not too busy (although that's rare) and give you a behind-the-scenes peek. Many will also allow prearranged field trips for elementary school classes.

Is There a Bagel Doctor in the House?

A sure sign of the nation's insatiable bagel appetite is readily apparent in, of all places, hospital emergency rooms. Doctors report that an increasing number of knife-wielding bagel lovers slice their bagels with such gusto that they slice their hands as well. Particularly on Saturday and Sunday mornings, hospital staffs brace themselves for an influx of bagel lacerations—no joke! They're considered to be among the most under-reported injuries.

Think of it. There could come a time when you'll have to buy Bagel Insurance. You'd be rated on how many bagels you eat a week and whether the texture is dense and knife-resistant or soft to the touch. Will you pay higher premiums if you eat your bagels with smoked salmon?

By the way, it's even being suggested that eating a bagel in the evening will help you sleep better. Now that's what you call one big sleeping pill.

Bagels Are Good for Your Love Life

The "teddy bear of foods," bagels bring out the best in everyone. Even the most unemotional people you know will wax poetic when you ask them what their favorite bagel flavor is!

Share a bagel and you have a friend for life. Business goes better with bagels. Arguments are more civilized over bagels and coffee. Making up is more loving with bagels and champagne. And if you want to make a lasting impression, forget the dozen roses. Just bring a dozen hot bagels and some cream cheese. You'll make a big hit and save a lot of money too.

CHAPTER 2

Bagel Styles of the Rich and Famous

News Bulletin:

The world's oldest-known cavemen billboard, just unearthed in Gatlinburg, Tennessee, reads,

"You can't get a decent bagel outside New York.
To order wholesale from Rocky in Brooklyn, dial One."

Whoopi Goldberg likes salted ones best and prefers them to pretzels. Paloma Picasso-Lopez credits them with inspiring her famed jewelry designs. Geraldo Rivera turns conservative when he acknowledges his favorites.

What is it that wields such power that it can tame a talk-on-the-wild-side TV host . . . mold sterling silver into ring-shaped signatures . . . cause a celebrated Hollywood star to pass up pretzels? Only The Bagel could make such a distinguished assemblage of glitterati react with wild abandon and practically weep with joy—in other words, go bonkers over bagels.

Occasionally, there's an exception. Don't look for legendary Broadway producer Hal Prince to create a bagel musical anytime soon. He's not a bagel devotee. He did note, however, that if I should consider changing my name to "Blueberry Muffin," I should recontact him.

Here's what the "Who's Who" of stage, film, television, fashion, food, sports, and law have to say when they bare their "roll" in the name of bagel lovers everywhere.

Jane Alexander

Chairperson of the National Endowment for the Arts, this highly acclaimed stage, television, and film actress is known for her memorable portrayals, but Jane's love of bagels is no act.

> *"I eat five or six bagels a week. I had my first bagel in 1960, and my favorite kind is plain—with the hole! My favorite way of eating them is with my teeth. I've tried all kinds of bagels, but I like plain ones the best. The strangest way I've ever eaten bagels is with refried beans. Why do I like bagels? They're chewy and exercise my jawline."*

Emanuel Ax

Since winning the first Arthur Rubinstein International Piano Competition in 1974, four-time Grammy Award–winner Emanuel Ax has become one of the leading pianists of his generation. Acclaimed for his mastery of Chopin, Mozart, Beethoven, and Dvořák, Emanuel's passion is playing a bagel *allegro agitato e energico* to a crescendo of cream cheese and onions.

> *"The first bagel I can recall eating was in the United States. I was 11 years old at the time and had just arrived from Poland. Bagels taste terrific, and I've enjoyed them ever since. I usually have four or five bagels a week, preferably sesame. I particularly like them with cream cheese and onions. I've even tried them with hummus and cheese."*

Letitia Baldrige

One of the most widely read authorities and author of thirteen books on social protocol and executive manners, Letitia first gained international recognition as chief of staff to Jacqueline Kennedy in the White House.

> *"I had my first bagel in New York when I was young, wrinkle-less, and naive. To me, bagels are the staff of life and remind me of the best of New York. Rye is my favorite. I usually have about five a week and prefer them spread with a tiny bit of low-fat margarine. I've gone so far as to anoint them with peanut butter with honey, which, proto-*

col aside, is 'yum-yum'! If I had to name my final meal before going to the electric chair, it would be a bagel and a hot fudge sundae."

Meredith Baxter

This versatile, talented actress enjoys her roles in front of the camera. But her favorite roll behind the scenes is a bagel!

"I love garlic and onion bagels. I first started eating bagels about thirty years ago and find their shape wonderfully appealing. I have three a week when I'm working, but none when I'm not. My favorite way of eating them is toasted very crisp—black on the edges—with scads of butter. For me, the strangest thing I've ever had on a bagel is cream cheese. I guess the reason I haven't experimented more with bagels is that I'm inhibited!"

David Brenner

A well-known comedian who always performs to packed houses, Brenner enjoys relaxing with well-packed bagels.

"I love eating my bagels (1) with my hands; (2) with thickly piled cream cheese and smooth peanut butter; (3) with cream cheese and tuna; (4) with cream cheese and crisp bacon. I especially love untoasted plain or pumpernickel bagels. I've been eating them since I was two months and three days old. On a good week I eat between 2,500 and 3,200."

Jane Brody

This noted cookbook author and *New York Times* "Personal Health" columnist is an expert on nutritious foods. That's why bagels are a mainstay in her breadbasket practically every day.

"I first started eating bagels somewhere between the ages of six months and a year old. My favorite kind is sesame seed. I eat about five to seven bagels a week. I prefer them au naturel. I simply break off chunks and eat them plain. The strangest combination I've

ever put on a bagel is caviar and sour cream—raising the bagel to new heights! I haven't done more experimenting because I like them just the way they come out of the oven. They're so chewy and satisfying."

Dr. Joyce Brothers

Dr. Joyce Brothers is a noted psychologist, radio and television personality, columnist, and author, whom millions of people rely on as a source of wisdom, common sense, and practical advice. According to Dr. Brothers, bagels play a significant "roll" in childhood.

"I first started eating bagels as an infant. My favorite kind of bagel is plain, and I eat a couple every week with cream cheese. Bagels are the best teething rings ever devised. They will keep a small child or infant, who's old enough to sit up and grasp an object, entertained and happy longer than anything else."

Dr. Leo F. Buscaglia

America's most endearing teacher, author, and lecturer, Dr. Leo Buscaglia helps people share in a better understanding of life and love. But his heart belongs to bagels—especially if he can hug one with lox and cream cheese.

"As a child, I grew up in a Jewish neighborhood and ate my first bagel in the home of my best friend, Sol. No one in my Italian family had ever heard of one, but I made them all converts. Sol's mother made bagels, and we began to call them Jewish doughnuts. I always got a bag as a reward for helping Sol's family on the Sabbath.

"Perhaps it's just the atmosphere, but there are no bagels in the world as good as those to be found in delis in New York! I especially enjoy plain bagels or, if I feel daring, poppy seed. I'll usually have two or three weekly, unless I'm in New York. Then I have them every day. When I was young and healthy, I loved bagels with lox and cream cheese. Later I ate them with only butter. Later still, I went to margarine and jams. Now I just eat them as they come. I like the texture, the feel, and the very unique taste. I've

tried pizza topping on a bagel, but it's not for me. Of course, even a lesser bagel is better than other alternatives."

Jerry Buss

Jerry Buss, real estate company executive and owner of the Los Angeles Lakers basketball team, says that although it's baskets that count on the court, off the court it's a basket of bagels.

"I first started eating bagels ten years ago. My favorite are raisin bagels, especially at breakfast time when they're toasted, spread with butter or cream cheese, and served with bacon and eggs. They taste so good that I have to limit myself."

Dick Clark

Creator, producer, and host of many of the country's most widely viewed television series and specials, and a driving force in American music, Clark gives bagels a "100"—they have a great beat and are fun to dance to.

"I first started eating bagels in the 1930s. My favorite kind is plain. I have one or two a week. I like them toasted with cream cheese. The strangest combination I've ever had on a bagel is peanut butter and pickles. I would experiment more, but I still bear a scar on the third finger of my left hand from a knife I used during an unsuccessful bagel experiment!!!"

Norm Crosby

This popular entertainer and wordsmith extraordinaire has a unique way of expressing himself. But ask Norm for a monologue on bagels, and he gives it to you straight.

"I started eating bagels when I was very young. I also played with them as a baby. They're difficult to chew with no teeth. I eat at least a half-dozen a week, especially pumpernickel. I like them toasted with cream cheese or open-face with tuna fish and a

slice of onion. Actually, I've tried everything on bagels—hot dogs, caviar (not together!), mustard—and I often make a pickle sandwich using bagels. I like bagels because they're quick to prepare, tasty, and good for you. If these sensible reasons aren't enough, I like 'em 'cause they're bagels and maybe because I don't like anything square!"

Hal David

Hal David's Academy Award–winning lyrics are as natural a combination with stage and screen blockbusters as bagels and cream cheese. From the prolific team of lyricist Hal David and composer Burt Bacharach came "Raindrops Keep Fallin' on My Head" (from the film *Butch Cassidy and the Sundance Kid*), "I'll Never Fall in Love Again" and "Promises, Promises" (from the Broadway musical *Promises, Promises*), "Alfie" (from the film *Alfie*), "Do You Know the Way to San Jose," "What the World Needs Now is Love," and "The Look of Love" (from the film *Casino Royale*), and dozens more hits. Though he admits he's never written an ode to the bagel, he's had plenty of inspiration. Even if it didn't win an Oscar, it would definitely win a Murray or a Sid.

> *"My love affair with bagels started when I was very young. My parents owned a deli in Brooklyn when I was a boy, and for years I thought that was the standard form of "bread." I'm a purist when it comes to bagels. I've tried rye, wheat, corn, raisin, sourdough, onion, cheese, pumpernickel, and even cinnamon, but my favorite is the plain water bagel—especially the bagels made with good old New York City water!*
>
> *"There's something very special about the taste of a real New York bagel. Perhaps it brings back my youth. But no matter where I've traveled, or where I've eaten a bagel, I can't wait to get back to New York for that first taste.*
>
> *"I usually eat a bagel for breakfast, just plain, with no topping on it. Of course I can easily be talked into adding slices of Nova and cream cheese, with perhaps a little onion, a slice of tomato, and some capers thrown over that. As you can see, I'm easy. If it's on the table in front of me, I usually eat it—especially bagels born and 'bread' in New York!"*

Fred de Cordova

De Cordova, who was the well-known producer-director of NBC's "The Tonight Show" starring Johnny Carson, thinks bagels have star quality. For Fred it's "Lights! Cameras! Bagels!"

"Why do I like bagels? Because bagels like me. I entered puberty with a bagel. That's when I first started eating them. Now my week wouldn't be complete without at least one. I would have experimented more with bagels if it hadn't been for parental warnings. Bagels can be habit-forming!"

Alan Dershowitz

If the truth were really known about Harvard Law School Professor Alan Dershowitz—defender of such headline-makers as O.J. Simpson, Claus von Bulow, Mike Tyson, and Leona Helmsley—he would rather be trying a garlic bagel than a court case.

"When I arrive at my office, I don't make a move until I synchronize my watch to the precise time that the garlic bagels will come out of the oven at the bagel bakery around the corner. In my legal opinion, what constitutes a great bagel is one I can eat right from the oven with nothing on it. Then I can enjoy its great taste and texture."

Phyllis Diller

A well-known comedienne and popular entertainer, Phyllis Diller has them rolling in the aisles with her repartee, and her observations about bagels are no exception.

"Even the thought of bagels is an inspiration to me. I bet you didn't know that when Ronald Reagan ran for president, he was so gung ho to get all the ethnic votes, he went into a deli and ordered a bagel. The waiter said, 'How would you like that?' Ronnie said, 'On rye.' Incidentally, my advice is never eat a day-old bagel. There is a day-old bagel someplace in this world with teeth in it—mine! By the way, did you hear about the new Bagel Diet? You just eat the holes."

Olympia Dukakis

This accomplished actress always delivers memorable performances in roles she can really sink her teeth into. But the starring roll she tackles with gusto is a bagel.

"I've been eating bagels for over thirty years. I like sesame best of all. I eat about three bagels a week. I guess you could say I'm a traditionalist at heart, because my favorite way of eating bagels is still with cream cheese and lox. However, I have gone so far as to have a bagel with banana, mayonnaise, and peanut butter on it. I love bagels because they're soft inside and have such a wonderful taste."

Whoopi Goldberg

Whoopi Goldberg, gifted Academy Award–winning actress and comedienne, has nourished her natural acting talents with years of bagel eating.

"I first started eating bagels as a kid in New York. I really like salted bagels the best. I have about four or five a week, usually toasted with butter. Bagels are great because they're chewy and satisfying! Who needs a pretzel when you have a bagel?"

Mark Goodson

The consummate innovative producer, Goodson has created many of television's most memorable, successful, and classic game shows, past and present, including "I've Got a Secret," "Beat the Clock," "The Price Is Right," and "Family Feud." Mark has absolutely no difficulty answering questions about bagels!

"I ate my first bagel in Sacramento—that sounds like the title of a song—when I was about ten. My favorite kind of bagel is good old-fashioned plain—with cream cheese (natch!) and smoked fish (natch!). No matter how many I eat, it's never enough. The strangest thing I've ever eaten on a bagel is caviar once, but I really haven't experimented because, bagel-wise, I'm a conservative. I like bagels because I love crusty things, and the taste of a bagel is redolent of my youth."

"As you can see, Dahling, I only do starring rolls . . ."

Heloise

This trusted "Dean of Household Hints" shares the suggestions of millions of fans in her widely read column, which appears in newspapers from coast to coast. Heloise will tell you that you should always have some bagels on hand, because no household is complete without them.

"Why do I like bagels? What's not to like!? I first started eating bagels in Washington, D.C., as a child. My favorite is whole wheat and, though I eat none when I'm in Texas, I eat as many as I can when I'm in New York. I like bagels with cream cheese, onion, and tomatoes, or peanut butter and cream cheese. Actually, nothing is too strange to put on a bagel."

Bob Hope

The premier Global Showman has faced millions of adoring fans the world over with ease. But he finds facing a bagel his greatest challenge.

"I remember the first time I ate a bagel. It was also the first time I broke a tooth. My favorite kind is a soft one, if it can be found. How many do I eat? Maybe one a year. My favorite way of eating them is with a doctor on hand. The strangest thing I've ever eaten on a bagel is vegetable soup. I haven't experimented more with bagels, because I prefer to eat doughnuts before they're soaked in cement. Why do I like bagels? . . . Why do I like the I.R.S.?"

Marty Ingels

Marty Ingels, a man of many talents—actor, comic, writer, and Hollywood Super Agent—always knows what's "in" and what's "out" . . . and, of course, the super-scoop on bagels. To quote the Brooklyn Boychik:

"Actually, it wasn't till I was fourteen that I realized they were edible. They were always piled up and stuck together in the freezer. My mother talked about keeping 'onions' in them . . . and 'seeds' . . . even 'water.' And we could only buy them on certain days

and only from a very fat man named Itzhak who dribbled when he spoke. Why would anyone want to eat one of those? (Once one of them fell out of the fridge onto my father's foot and broke two of his toes. Most kids I knew were scared of them.)

"They were much easier to digest when I was a kid. Got a very sensitive stomach these days, so I take them intravenously. And people really differ on their health effect. My doctor once told me that he put absolutely no limit on the number of bagels he himself ate. But last week his widow left a message on my service to call her about that. And people like them with different things—with butter, with cheese, with lox, even with meat. I like mine with an ambulance. Somebody once asked me what was the strangest combination I ever put on a bagel. I once put a twenty-eight-year-old hooker named Beulah on one and turned the lights out. (She now lives on a kibbutz just south of Haifa, and they say she's doing very well.) For a while, I tried "experimenting" with bagels, but I lost the grant.

"Why do I like bagels?—No jokes? Because they bring me back to a sweeter, simpler time when good was good and bad was bad and right was right and wrong was wrong and we may not've known a hell of a lot, but we knew which was which and when. Today I'm not sure of anyone—or anything—except my bagel."

Shirley Jones Ingels

Shirley Jones, America's sweetheart, whose Oscar-winning career has included the movies *Oklahoma!, Carousel, The Music Man,* and *Elmer Gantry* and the long-running television series "The Partridge Family," confides that she deserves an Oscar for living with husband Marty . . . and eating bagels.

"I first started eating bagels in 1977. Marty wrote it into our prenuptial agreement after he saw me order corned beef with mayonnaise. How many bagels do I eat a week? That depends on how often my in-laws visit (and how much mayonnaise I have in the house). My favorite way of eating bagels is with communion wafers. But the most gratifying combination I've ever put on a bagel is Bromo and Maalox. I haven't exper-

imented with bagels because Marty said something about how eating them with any-one other than your husband constitutes some sort of Hebrew adultery. Why do I like bagels? I've lived long enough."

Larry King

America's favorite television and radio talk-show host has been a bagel eater since birth. He really knows what he likes. Besides, bagels don't talk back!

"Bagels have a taste all their own. They are perfectly named: They fill, they bring plea-sure—they are bagels! *I eat about five or six a week. I especially like salt bagels. My favorite way of eating them is with lox and cream cheese. All others are frauds."*

Ed McMahon

Now host of the syndicated program "Star Search," Ed McMahon was for many years television's most celebrated sidekick while on "The Tonight Show" starring Johnny Carson. What else would you expect Ed to say about his favorite bagel but *"Heeere's onion!"*

"Onion bagels are number one with me. I eat three or four a week. I first started eat-ing bagels while in the service during World War II. My favorite way of eating them is toasted with peanut butter or cream cheese and lox. I haven't tried other combina-tions because of my inherent shyness. Why do I like bagels? Because they're delicious! What better reason?"

Marvin Mitchelson

This famed palimony and divorce attorney to the stars says the splits he *really* likes to work on are two bagel halves.

"I've been eating bagels for over forty years. My favorite kind is pumpernickel. I usually eat from two to five a week and love them hollowed out, with lox, onion, and whitefish—

no cream cheese. The strangest combination I've ever had on a bagel is banana and cottage cheese. Why do I like bagels? The indefinable feeling of being Jewish."

John Moschitta, Jr.

John Moschitta is the uniquely talented television personality who began fast-talking his way into millions of American living rooms with his memorable commercials for Federal Express. The faster John speaks, the more time he has to eat bagels nice and slow!

"You never forget your first bagel. I had mine on Tuesday, July 14, 1957, at 10:07 A.M. My favorite kind is poppy seed. I have two a week. The strangest combination I've ever had on a bagel is pineapple with spaghetti sauce. But my all-time favorite way of eating bagels is with chopped liver, turkey, coleslaw, Muenster cheese, lettuce, and tomato. I call it the 'mighty mouthful!' Bagels taste great any time and any way, plus you can play ring-toss with them."

John Offerdahl

Former All-Pro linebacker with the Miami Dolphins, John Offerdahl exchanged his football salary for bagel dough. He owns Offerdahl's Bagel Gourmet, a popular chain of bagel bakeries headquartered in South Florida.

"When I was a child, Mom bought frozen bagels at the store, toasted them, and topped them with cream cheese and fresh fruit. I've loved them ever since. These days I prefer a fresh seven-grain or multigrain bagel with a light smear of honey butter seven days a week—a touchdown! What else would you expect from a former football pro turned bagel pro?

"Bagels have such good texture, and they're good for you—healthy with no fat. They even have a clean aftertaste. No lingering reminder an hour later. The bagel itself makes me smile. Who would have thought this shy holey fellow would take centuries of *grooming before he could make his grand entrance in stores across the world. Here's a 'toasted' bagel for the 21st century!"*

Paloma Picasso-Lopez

This world-class designer and savvy businesswoman heads a signature line that includes jewelry, scarves, handbags, perfume, cosmetics, china, crystal, and silver. She credits bagels as her inspiration.

> *"Since I am French, I did not grow up on bagels, but I had my first one in 1968. My favorite kind is plain. It's difficult to say how many I eat a week, because I don't spend that much time in America. Besides, I am always on a diet! I particularly enjoy eating bagels with smoked Scottish salmon. The strangest combination I've ever had on a bagel is mashed potatoes on a bed of lettuce with olive-oil vinaigrette. I would be even more inventive if I had more free time and did less dieting. I'm afraid of all the good things I can create. Why do I like bagels? Because of the taste and the look. You might notice there is a similarity—a definite connection—between my designs and bagels."*

Sally Jessy Raphael

One of the elite group of television talk-show hosts who are so well known they needn't use their last names, Sally is a bagel-lover who discovered bagels on the Island. Not Manhattan, but Puerto Rico.

> *"I had my first bagels in Puerto Rico. They came frozen from Pueblo Supermarkets, and the island went bonkers over bagels. What a combination—rice, beans, and bagels! Now my favorite combination is with cream cheese and salty Norwegian salmon. Plain bagels are* numero uno *for me. I usually have two-and-a-half each week. The best news is they're chewy and not fattening. Figuring I'd substitute one white thing for another, I tried mayo instead of cream cheese, with my salmon. I've also used chocolate spread on bagels. Here's a creative idea for you. I discovered that bagels are good*

to use for decorating your Christmas tree. The hole's already there. Just tie a green or red bow through each one and deck the halls with boughs of bagels!"

Ahmad Rashad

Ahmad Rashad, popular member of the NBC Sports broadcast team, was also a star football player for the Minnesota Vikings. But he fills *his* super bowl with bagels.

> "I'm a basic, uncomplicated kind of guy. As a snack, I like my bagels not toasted with grape jelly and cream cheese. As a real meal, I like them toasted with cream cheese and grape jelly."

Phyllis Richman

Restaurant critic for *The Washington Post,* Phyllis Richman is a bagel purist. She started eating bagels as soon as she had teeth, and she's been giving them critical acclaim ever since.

> "My favorite kind of bagel is a good one. But I won't tell you how many I eat a week. That's top secret! Now as to how I like eating them . . . is there any other way than with Nova and cream cheese? You don't mess around with perfection! Why do I like bagels? That's like asking why I like breathing!"

Geraldo Rivera

Geraldo Rivera, controversial and widely viewed talk-show host, is well known for his penetrating style and investigative reporting. Geraldo investigated his first bagel more than twenty years ago and has been enthusiastically digging into the subject ever since.

> "I started eating bagels around 1965 when I moved to New York after college. My favorite kind is poppy seed. I eat two or three a week, either toasted or untoasted, with cream cheese and olives—olives in between the bagel and the cream cheese. The strangest thing I've ever eaten on a bagel is not so strange at all—raisins. I'm very con-

servative about my culinary adventures, so I haven't experimented more. Why do I like bagels? They are tastier, funnier, and more creative than plain bread. And they taste great with cream cheese and olives!"

Joan Rivers

This popular comedienne is never at a loss for words, especially about bagels.

"I first started eating bagels when I was twenty minutes old. That's when I had a bagel and a Hershey bar! My favorite bagels are the ones with the hole in the center. I love all varieties. How many do I eat a week? I stop counting after Tuesday. My favorite way of eating a bagel is as a sandwich, filled with a pepperoni pizza. The strangest thing I've ever eaten on a bagel is a banana split. Why do I like bagels? They seem to like me. They go right to my thighs and just won't leave."

Phil Rizzuto

Baseball Hall-of-Famer Phil Rizzuto, one of the most popular Yankees of all time, was for years the team's most widely recognized broadcaster. When Phil rounds the plate, there's always a bagel on it. Holy cow!

"I eat at least a half-dozen bagels a week. I've been eating bagels ever since 1937. My favorite kinds are salt and plain, with cream cheese, lox, and chive cheese. The strangest combination I've ever had on a bagel is jelly, bananas, and cream cheese. Why do I like bagels? They're the best, especially in the morning and late evening."

RORY

Singer, composer, and host of her own television series on the Learning Channel, Sony Wonder recording artist RORY is one of the entertainment world's most popular performers of children's music. She blends pop, jazz, blues, and oldies, but her favorite combo is a bagel with cream cheese, a really juicy red-tomato slice, lots of fresh ground pepper, and a little salt.

> *"My dad, whom I adored, was a longtime Washington, D.C., physician who had a very special relationship with many of his patients. Two of them, Mr. and Mrs. Hinkle, owned Hinkle's Bakery on Georgia Avenue. Late at night, Dad would take us to see the Hinkles. My two sisters and I were always ushered into the back by Mr. Hinkle, who was wearing his long white apron, his skin whitened by flour. He'd make us bagel bracelets, twisting the dough around our wrists. We were delighted. Our special treat was to snack on hot bagels coming out of the oven. Bagels have never been quite the same for me since. I also remember our visits to our New York City relatives. Each Sunday we had a great brunch of bagels, fish, the works! We'd make what we called a 'Dagwood,' which was a bagel with cream cheese, kippered salmon, tomato, and cucumber. We'd stack 'em up and see if we could fit the whole thing in our mouth for the first bite. I guess you could say that bagels are a real part of me."*

Willard Scott

NBC "Today Show" personality Willard Scott is America's favorite weatherman. According to Willard, the national radar weather map picks up bagels from coast to coast.

> *"Today's forecast is a sesame-seed bagel, my favorite kind! Take it from ol' Willard, bagels are the greatest. Especially sesame bagels piled high with cream cheese. I eat them every chance I get. Now if I could only figure out how to grow bagels on my farm!"*

Doc Severinsen

Famed concert artist and for years the music director of "The Tonight Show" band on NBC-TV, Doc admits to putting down his trumpet for a bagel.

> *"My favorite bagel arrangement is ham on an egg bagel. I've found that bagels are not only high in food value, they're also useful for construction purposes."*

Artie Shaw

This legendary clarinet virtuoso, bandleader, and arranger says that bagels have been music to his ears for years!

> "I first started eating bagels sometime before or during the first Crusade. I love onion bagels, sesame bagels, plain bagels—any kind at all, just so it's a bagel. How many do I eat? About six or eight a week. I usually have them toasted with butter. Why, is there any other way? I'm your basic straight-ahead bagel type—nothing strange, nothing kinky. Asking me why I like bagels is like asking why I like breathing air or drinking water. All bagels are good and good for you, too. So what's not to like?"

Liz Smith

The widely read syndicated show-biz columnist of *Newsday* knows bagels make good press, especially with cream cheese.

> "I had never even seen a bagel until 1949 when I came to New York and had my first one. I've tried peanut butter on bagels but haven't experimented more because I'm too gentile and cowardly. I love sesame bagels and would eat more of them, but I have to ration myself! My favorite way to eat a bagel is toasted with lots of butter and cream cheese. Bagels are delicious and a challenge to eat."

Abigail Van Buren

Abigail Van Buren, whose syndicated "Dear Abby" advice column is read and followed by millions of devoted readers, advises you to eat at least one bagel every day.

> "I've been eating bagels ever since I had teeth. My favorite kind is an egg bagel. I go on sporadic bagel binges and eat bagels every day for a week. Then I knock off for a while. My favorite way of eating a bagel is to slice it lengthwise, toast it, and load on the butter and cream cheese. I've also enjoyed caviar on bagels—a very expensive frivolity indeed, but worth it! I haven't experimented more because I'm happy with my present mode of eating bagels. I love them because they're delicious. Why else?"

Diane Von Furstenberg

This well-known designer, who heads one of the country's most successful dressmaking companies, is responsible for putting the "little print wrap dress" in the closet of every fashion-conscious woman in America. But what she enjoys wrapping her hands around is a bagel.

> *"I first started eating bagels when I was a child. I like bagels because they remind me of my father. They are cozy like little pillows."*

Duke Zeibert

He's hosted many of the most powerful people in the nation's capital. Perennial restaurateur Duke Zeibert is also a "roll-model" for bagel lovers everywhere.

> *"I eat bagels every day of the week, especially pumpernickel with cream cheese and mustard. I've been eating bagels for so many years now, I can't recall. Bagels give me wisdom and strength. Let's face it. How else could I settle petty differences between the chef, pastry chef, roll baker, and head waiter—and try to keep them all?"*

CHAPTER 3

Handling and Storing Bagels

Do you know that camels get their humps from storing bags of bagels that are air-dropped in the desert by a New York deli?

You can eat bagels any way you like—toasted, heated, or fresh from the bag. Everybody quickly develops a personal style. Some people only eat bagels toasted; others think it's heresy to toast them. Some cut them in half; others only eat them whole. And that's just for starters—it doesn't include all the individual flavor preferences!

Any way you slice them, bagels are a deliciously versatile experience. They sit up tall, proud, and golden-brown, waiting to be sliced, spread, topped, or scooped out and filled.

If you buy your bagels at a bakery where they're continuously baked, you'll often get them hot from the oven. If you're buying more than you plan to eat the same day, simply freeze the rest. If they're still hot, let them cool first before transferring them to plastic bags for freezing. This prevents them from getting soggy.

Cut your bagels in half before freezing them so you'll have the option of enjoying a whole or half bagel whenever the mood strikes. You can toast your bagels frozen, or if you like them heated rather than toasted, put them in the oven or toaster oven for five minutes at 400°.

Lox, stocked, and bageled

You can freshen days-old bagels by putting them in a covered pot with a few drops of water and placing the pot in a preheated 350° oven for ten minutes or so. But frankly, it makes much more sense to freeze bagels instead of letting them sit around . . . unless you want to use them for paperweights, doorstops, or hockey pucks, or give them to the dog!

Toaster manufacturers have become quite accommodating to bagel lovers. They've come out with toaster models with larger-than-standard-size openings, so you might want to be on the lookout for one of these. If you have a toaster oven, all the better. It makes toasting or heating a snap no matter how big your bagels are.

Be aware that heating bagels in the microwave oven changes their consistency, making them somewhat rubbery. Use a microwave as a last resort, heating bagels for just a few seconds at a time. You *can* use the microwave to *defrost* frozen bagels successfully (fifty seconds on the DEFROST setting).

Please note that many of the recipes in this book call for the use of a foil-covered cookie sheet. This makes for quick and easy cleanup. Once you remove the aluminum foil, your cookie sheet is instantly clean.

CHAPTER 4

Marilyn's Easy-Make Bagels in Under 90 Minutes

Two space creatures overheard talking:

"Earthlings swear by their garlic bagels.
A lot they know — Manny's on Jupiter has the biggest!"

For crusty, chewy bagels you can bake with ease in your own kitchen, try these all-new and improved recipes from my personal collection. Even if you've never baked bread, you can successfully make homemade bagels. Think of these as your #1 home-bagel recipes. All the ingredients are mixed in *one* bowl. Each recipe requires just *one* brief rising period. And once you take these bagels from the oven, you'll definitely want more than *one*.

Two of my recipes use whole-wheat flour, which has great nutritional value, and five call for bread flour, a high-gluten flour that results in greater protein content, longer shelf life, bigger volume, and better shaping and rising. Both flours are available on supermarket shelves. For the uninitiated, bread flour contains more gluten than does regular enriched flour. Gluten is a protein structure in wheat. The gluten in bread flour is developed when you add water and knead it.

Words of advice before you begin: Use liquid measuring cups to measure water and dry measuring cups to measure flour. When measuring flour, dip the cup into the flour and use a knife to level off the excess. Bagels made with whole-wheat flour have a denser texture; that's why the amount of flour in those recipes is less than in my recipes that use bread flour. The bagels rise only partially during preparation, because the rising time is shorter than in typical bread recipes. When the bagels are placed in boiling water during the kettling stage, however, they complete the rise and puff up. You may find that your bagel dough is stickier on high-humidity days or in a warm kitchen. If the dough remains sticky and elastic even after rising, it will still hold up just fine in the boiling-water stage without falling apart.

Marilyn's Basic Bagels

Make an assortment of plain, poppy seed, sesame, garlic, onion, whatever you prefer.

> 2 cups water, warm to the touch
>
> 1 tablespoon active dry yeast
>
> 4 tablespoons barley malt syrup
>
> 2 teaspoons salt
>
> 5 cups bread flour
>
> 3 quarts water
>
> Sesame seeds, poppy seeds, dehydrated or fresh minced garlic or onion
>
> Yellow cornmeal

1. In large bowl, combine warm water and yeast and stir until dissolved. Add 2 tablespoons barley malt syrup, and salt. Mix until all ingredients are thoroughly blended.

2. Add bread flour. Mix until ingredients are blended.

3. Place dough on a lightly bread-floured surface and begin to knead it. If the dough is sticky, add very small amounts of bread flour as necesssary. It's better to add less than more. To be sure you don't add too much at a time, dip your hands in the flour, shake off the excess, and knead. Repeat as necessary. Knead the dough vigorously for 12 minutes.

4. When finished, use a sharp knife to cut the dough into twelve equal parts.

5. Take a section of dough and roll it in your palms to make a ball. Poke your thumbs through the center and work them around to make a hole a bit larger than the size of a quarter. Repeat with remaining eleven sections. Place the formed bagels on a bread-floured work surface about 2 inches apart. Be sure there are no cool drafts directly on them.

6. Cover them with a clean dish towel and let them rise for 25 minutes.

7. Meanwhile add the remaining 2 tablespoons barley malt syrup to 3 quarts water in a large pot, and bring to a boil. Preheat the oven to 450°. Prepare your cookie sheet or pan by lightly sprinkling it with cornmeal.

8. At the end of 25 minutes, you're ready to place your bagels in the boiling water, four bagels at a time. This stage is called *kettling*. The perfect bagel, when kettled, should quickly sink to the bottom of the pot of boiling water and rise immediately. Boil for about 4 minutes, turning the bagels over frequently with a slotted spoon. If your bagels don't sink to the bottom when you first put them in the pot, don't worry. However, if they sink to the bottom and lie there, wait till they rise to the top (and they will) before timing the 4 minutes.

9. After kettling, remove the bagels from the water with a slotted spoon, allowing any excess water to drain off. Place them close together with edges touching on your cornmeal-prepared cookie sheet or pan. Liberally sprinkle the bagels with your favorite toppings. For an assortment, make some poppy seed, sesame seed, plain, garlic, and onion. Or combine all the toppings and make an "everything" bagel.

10. Place pan on rack in middle of oven and bake for 20 minutes. Check the bagels by looking at their color; if necessary, continue baking until golden. Watch the bagels carefully toward the end of the baking time because every oven is different, and yours may brown quickly. After taking them out of the oven, remove the bagels from the cookie sheet and let them cool on a wire rack for 10 minutes.

Note: Barley malt syrup is a natural sweetener available at health food stores; if you've refrigerated it, let it come to room temperature before using or microwave it very briefly on low to remove the chill.

Makes 12 bagels

Marilyn's Whole-Wheat Granola Bagels

A whole-wheat treat with a touch of sweet.

> 2 cups water, warm to the touch
> 1 tablespoon active dry yeast
> 5 tablespoons barley malt syrup
> 2 teaspoons salt
> 1 1/4 cups nonfat granola
> 1/3 cup golden raisins
> 2 1/4 cups whole-wheat flour
> 1 1/2 cups bread flour
> 3 quarts water
> Yellow cornmeal

1. In large bowl, combine warm water and yeast and stir until dissolved. Add 2 tablespoons barley malt syrup, and salt. Mix until all ingredients are thoroughly blended.

2. Add granola and raisins and mix well. Then add whole-wheat flour and 1 1/4 cups bread flour and mix until blended. If the dough looks loose, add remaining 1/4 cup bread flour and blend well.

3. Place dough on a lightly bread-floured surface and begin to knead it. If the dough is sticky, add very small amounts of bread flour as necesssary. It's better to add less than more, especially when working with whole-wheat flour. To be sure you don't add too much at a time, simply dip your hands in the bread flour, shake off the excess, and knead. Repeat as necessary. Knead the dough vigorously for 12 minutes.

4. When finished, use a sharp knife to cut the dough into twelve equal parts.

5. Take a section of dough and roll it in your palms to make a ball. Poke your thumbs through the center and work them around to make a hole a bit larger than the size of a quarter. Repeat with remaining eleven sections. Place the formed bagels on a bread-floured work surface about 2 inches apart. Be sure there are no cool drafts directly on them.

6. Cover them with a clean dish towel and let them rise for 25 minutes.

7. Meanwhile add the remaining 3 tablespoons barley malt syrup to 3 quarts water in a large pot, and bring to a boil. Preheat the oven to 450°. Prepare your cookie sheet or pan by lightly sprinkling it with cornmeal.

8. At the end of 25 minutes, you're ready to place your bagels in the boiling water, four bagels at a time. This stage is called *kettling*. The perfect bagel, when kettled, should quickly sink to the bottom of the pot of boiling water and rise immediately. Boil for about 4 minutes, turning the bagels over frequently with a slotted spoon. If your bagels don't sink to the bottom when you first put them in the pot, don't worry. However, if they sink to the bottom and lie there, wait till they rise to the top (and they will) before timing the 4 minutes.

9. After kettling, remove the bagels from the water with a slotted spoon, allowing any excess water to drain off. Place them close together with edges touching on your cornmeal-prepared cookie sheet.

10. Place pan on rack in middle of oven and bake for 20 minutes. Check the bagels by looking at their color; if necessary, continue baking until golden. Watch the bagels carefully

toward the end of the baking time because every oven is different and yours may brown quickly. After taking them out of the oven, remove the bagels from the cookie sheet and let them cool on a wire rack for 10 minutes.

Note: Barley malt syrup is a natural sweetener available at health food stores; if you've refrigerated it, let it come to room temperature before using or microwave it very briefly on low to remove the chill.

Makes 12 bagels

Marilyn's Cheese Duo Bagels

This is a luscious blend of Parmesan and Romano cheeses with fresh dill.

2 cups water, warm to the touch
1 tablespoon active dry yeast
4 tablespoons barley malt syrup
2 teaspoons salt
4 cups bread flour
1/2 cup freshly grated Parmesan cheese
1/2 cup freshly grated Romano cheese
1/8 teaspoon black pepper
1 tablespoon finely chopped fresh dill
3 quarts water
Yellow cornmeal

1. In large bowl, combine warm water and yeast and stir until dissolved. Add 2 tablespoons barley malt syrup, and salt. Mix until all ingredients are thoroughly blended.

2. Add bread flour, both cheeses, pepper and dill. Mix until ingredients are well blended.

3. Place dough on a lightly bread-floured surface and begin to knead it. If the dough is sticky, add very small amounts of bread flour as necesssary. It's better to add less than more. If you want to be sure you don't add too much at a time, dip your hands in the flour, shake off the excess, and knead. Repeat as necessary. Knead the dough vigorously for 12 minutes.

4. When finished, use a sharp knife to cut the dough into twelve equal parts.

5. Take a section of dough and roll it in your palms to make a ball. Poke your thumbs through the center and work them around to make a hole a bit larger than the size of a quarter. Repeat with remaining eleven sections. Place the formed bagels on a bread-floured work surface about 2 inches apart. Be sure there are no cool drafts directly on them.

6. Cover them with a clean dish towel and let them rise for 25 minutes.

7. Meanwhile add the remaining 2 tablespoons barley malt syrup to 3 quarts water in a large pot, and bring to a boil. Preheat the oven to 450°. Prepare your cookie sheet or pan by lightly sprinkling it with cornmeal.

8. At the end of 25 minutes, you're ready to place your bagels in the boiling water, four bagels at a time. This stage is called *kettling.* The perfect bagel, when kettled, should quickly sink to the bottom of the pot of boiling water and rise immediately. Boil for about 4 minutes, turning the bagels over frequently with a slotted spoon. If your bagels don't sink to the bottom when you first put them in the pot, don't worry. However, if they sink to the bottom and lie there, wait till they rise to the top (and they will) before timing the 4 minutes.

9. After kettling, remove the bagels from the water with a slotted spoon, allowing any excess water to drain off. Place them close together with edges touching on your cornmeal-prepared cookie sheet or pan.

10. Place pan on rack in middle of oven and bake for 20 minutes. Check the bagels by looking at their color; if necessary, continue baking until golden. Watch the bagels carefully

toward the end of the baking time because every oven is different and yours may brown quickly. After taking them out of the oven, remove the bagels from the cookie sheet and let them cool on a wire rack for 10 minutes.

Makes 12 bagels

To make a triple-cheese version, top each bagel with a slice of mozzarella or provolone cheese and continue baking or until cheese melts.

Note: Barley malt syrup is a natural sweetener available at health food stores; if you've refrigerated it, let it come to room temperature before using or microwave it very briefly on low to remove the chill.

Marilyn's Best Blueberry Bagels

Natural blueberry fruit syrup with no added sugar makes these delicious and healthful.

1 1/4 cups water, warm to the touch
1 tablespoon active dry yeast
5 tablespoons barley malt syrup
1 cup blueberry fruit syrup (all fruit, no added sugar), at room temperature
2 teaspoons salt
5 cups bread flour
3 quarts water
Yellow cornmeal

1. In large bowl, combine warm water and yeast and stir until dissolved. Add 2 tablespoons barley malt syrup, blueberry fruit syrup, and salt. Mix until all ingredients are thoroughly blended.

2. Add bread flour and mix. Because of the fruit syrup, the dough will be particularly sticky.

3. Place dough on a lightly bread-floured surface and begin to knead it. If the dough is sticky, add very small amounts of bread flour as necesssary. It's better to add less than more. To be sure you don't add too much at a time, dip your hands in the flour, shake off the excess, and knead. Repeat as necessary. Knead the dough vigorously for 12 minutes.

4. When finished, use a sharp knife to cut the dough into twelve equal parts.

5. Take a section of dough and roll it in your palms to make a ball. Poke your thumbs through the center and work them around to make a hole a bit larger than the size of a quarter. Repeat with remaining eleven sections. Place the formed bagels on a bread-floured work surface about 2 inches apart. Be sure there are no cool drafts directly on them.

6. Cover them with a clean dish towel and let them rise for 25 minutes.

7. Meanwhile, add the remaining 3 tablespoons barley malt syrup to 3 quarts water in a large pot and bring to a boil. Preheat the oven to 450°. Prepare your cookie sheet or pan by lightly sprinkling it with cornmeal.

8. At the end of 25 minutes, you're ready to place your bagels in the boiling water, four bagels at a time. This stage is called *kettling*. The perfect bagel, when kettled, should quickly sink to the bottom of the pot of boiling water and rise immediately. Boil for about 4 minutes, turning the bagels over frequently with a slotted spoon. If your bagels don't sink to the bottom when you first put them in the pot, don't worry. However, if they sink to the bottom and lie there, wait till they rise to the top (and they will) before timing the 4 minutes.

9. After kettling, remove the bagels from the water with a slotted spoon, allowing any excess water to drain off. Place them close together with edges touching on your cornmeal-prepared cookie sheet or pan.

10. Place pan on rack in middle of oven and bake for 20 minutes. Check the bagels by looking at their color; if necessary, continue baking until golden. Watch the bagels carefully

toward the end of the baking time because every oven is different and yours may brown quickly. After taking them out of the oven, remove the bagels from the cookie sheet and let them cool on a wire rack for 10 minutes.

Makes 12 bagels

Note: Barley malt syrup is a natural sweetener available at health food stores; if you've refrigerated it, let it come to room temperature before using or microwave it very briefly on low to remove the chill.

Marilyn's Sesame Whole-Wheat Bagels

A coat of sesame seeds adds a tasty crunch.

2 cups water, warm to the touch
1 tablespoon active dry yeast
5 tablespoons barley malt syrup
2 teaspoons salt
3 cups whole-wheat flour
1 1/4 cups bread flour
3 quarts water
Yellow cornmeal
Sesame seeds

1. In large bowl, combine warm water and yeast and stir until dissolved. Add 2 tablespoons barley malt syrup, and salt. Mix until all ingredients are thoroughly blended.

2. Add whole-wheat flour and bread flour. Mix until blended.

3. Place dough on a lightly bread-floured surface and begin to knead it. If the dough is sticky, add very small amounts of bread flour as necesssary. It's better to add less than more, especially when working with whole-wheat flour. To be sure you don't add too much at a time, dip your hands in the bread flour, shake off the excess, and knead. Repeat as necessary. Knead the dough vigorously for 12 minutes.

4. When finished, use a sharp knife to cut the dough into twelve equal parts.

5. Take a section of dough and roll it in your palms to make a ball. Poke your thumbs through the center and work them around to make a hole a bit larger than the size of a quarter. Repeat with remaining eleven sections. Place the formed bagels on a bread-floured work surface about 2 inches apart. Be sure there are no cool drafts directly on them.

6. Cover them with a clean dish towel and let them rise for 25 minutes.

7. Meanwhile add the remaining 3 tablespoons barley malt syrup to 3 quarts water in a large pot, and bring to a boil. Preheat the oven to 450°. Prepare your cookie sheet or pan by lightly sprinkling it with cornmeal.

8. At the end of 25 minutes, you're ready to place your bagels in the boiling water, four bagels at a time. This stage is called *kettling*. The perfect bagel, when kettled, should quickly sink to the bottom of the pot of boiling water and rise immediately. Boil for about 4 minutes, turning the bagels over frequently with a slotted spoon. If your bagels don't sink to the bottom when you first put them in the pot, don't worry. However, if they sink to the bottom and lie there, wait till they rise to the top (and they will) before timing the 4 minutes.

9. After kettling, remove the bagels from the water with a slotted spoon, allowing any excess water to drain off. Place them close together with edges touching on your corn-meal-prepared cookie sheet or pan.

10. Liberally sprinkle bagels with sesame seeds.

11. Place pan on rack in middle of oven and bake for 20 minutes. Check the bagels by looking at their color; if necessary, continue baking until golden. Watch the bagels carefully toward the end of the baking time because every oven is different and yours may brown quickly. After taking them out of the oven, remove the bagels from the cookie sheet and let them cool on a wire rack for 10 minutes.

Makes 12 bagels

Note: Barley malt syrup is a natural sweetener available at health food stores; if you've refrigerated it, let it come to room temperature before using or microwave it very briefly on low to remove the chill.

Marilyn's Strawberry Pink Valentine Bagels

Make every day Valentine's Day.

> 1 1/4 cups water, warm to the touch
> 1 tablespoon active dry yeast
> 5 tablespoons barley malt syrup
> 1 cup natural strawberry fruit syrup (all fruit, no added sugar)
>   at room temperature
> 2 teaspoons salt
> 5 cups bread flour
> 3 quarts water
> Yellow cornmeal

1. In large bowl, combine warm water and yeast and stir until dissolved. Add 2 tablespoons barley malt syrup, strawberry fruit syrup, and salt. Mix until all ingredients are thoroughly blended.

2. Add bread flour and mix until blended. Because of the fruit syrup, the dough will be particularly sticky.

3. Place dough on a lightly bread-floured surface and begin to knead it. If the dough is sticky, add very small amounts of bread flour as necessary. It's better to add less than more. To be sure you don't add too much at a time, dip your hands in the flour, shake off the excess, and knead. Repeat as necessary. Knead the dough vigorously for 12 minutes.

4. When finished, use a sharp knife to cut the dough into twelve equal parts.

5. Take a section of dough and roll it on your work surface until it is a 10-to-12-inch-long rod (instead of rolling it in your palms to make a ball) (see diagram A). *Throughout step #5, be sure to use your flat work surface to form your heart-shaped bagels.* Fold the rod in half to determine the midpoint (see diagram B). That will be the indentation at the top of the heart, so form a V-shaped depression at this point. Then shape the rod sections around to form a heart with a heart-shaped hole in the middle (see diagram C). Join the ends of the dough securely to make the heart's pointed bottom. Repeat with remaining eleven sections. Place the heart-shaped bagels on a bread-floured work surface about 2 inches apart. Be sure there are no cool drafts directly on them.

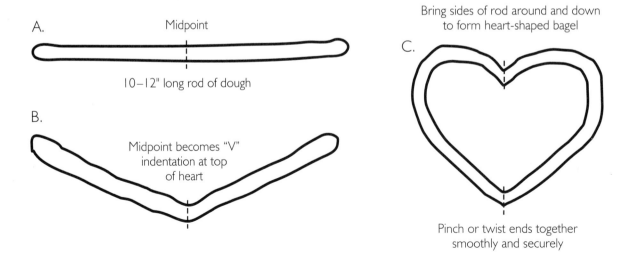

A.
Midpoint
10–12" long rod of dough

B.
Midpoint becomes "V" indentation at top of heart

C.
Bring sides of rod around and down to form heart-shaped bagel
Pinch or twist ends together smoothly and securely

6. Cover them with a clean dish towel and let them rise for 25 minutes.

7. Meanwhile, add the remaining 3 tablespoons barley malt syrup to 3 quarts water in a large pot and bring to a boil. Preheat the oven to 450°. Prepare your cookie sheet or pan by lightly sprinkling it with cornmeal.

8. At the end of 25 minutes, you're ready to place your bagels in the boiling water, four bagels at a time. This stage is called *kettling*. The perfect bagel, when kettled, should quickly sink to the bottom of the pot of boiling water and rise immediately. Boil for about 4 minutes, turning the bagels over frequently with a slotted spoon. If your bagels don't sink to the bottom when you first put them in the pot, don't worry. However, if they sink to the bottom and lie there, wait till they rise to the top (and they will) before timing the 4 minutes.

9. After kettling, remove the bagels from the water with a slotted spoon, allowing any excess water to drain off. Place them close together with edges touching on your cornmeal-prepared cookie sheet or pan.

10. Place pan on rack in middle of oven and bake for 20 minutes. Check the bagels by looking at their color; if necessary, continue baking until golden. Watch the bagels carefully toward the end of the baking time because every oven is different and yours may brown quickly. After taking them out of the oven, remove the bagels from the cookie sheet and let them cool on a wire rack for 10 minutes.

Makes 12 bagels

Note: Barley malt syrup is a natural sweetener available at health food stores; if you've refrigerated it, let it come to room temperature before using or microwave it very briefly on low to remove the chill.

Marilyn's Vegetable Garden Bagels

Vegetables in the dough make a well-rounded combo. This recipe takes a bit longer than 90 minutes because of the added prep time for the vegetables.

> 1/4 cup very finely chopped or shredded carrots
>
> 1/4 cup very finely chopped sweet red pepper
>
> 1/4 cup very finely chopped fresh parsley or watercress
>
> 1/4 cup very finely chopped mushrooms
>
> 2 tablespoons water
>
> 1 1/2 cups warm water mixed with dehydrated natural vegetable broth
>   mix (no added salt); follow package directions for proportions
>
> 1 tablespoon active dry yeast
>
> 4 tablespoons barley malt syrup
>
> 2 teaspoons salt
>
> 5 cups bread flour
>
> 3 quarts water
>
> Yellow cornmeal

1. Place carrots, red pepper, parsley or watercress, and mushrooms in a microwave-safe dish and stir. Add 2 tablespoons water, cover, and microwave 3 minutes. Drain vegetables, reserving liquid, which will probably amount to about 3/4 cup. Set vegetables aside for the moment.

2. In large bowl, combine warm reserved vegetable liquid with prepared vegetable broth to equal 2 cups. Add yeast and stir till dissolved. Add 2 tablespoons barley malt syrup, and salt. Mix until all ingredients are thoroughly blended.

3. Add bread flour and cooked vegetables. Mix until blended.

4. Place dough on a lightly bread-floured surface and begin to knead it. The dough will probably be sticky because the cooked vegetables themselves add liquid. Add very small amounts of bread flour as necesssary. It's better to use less than more. To be sure you don't add too much at a time, simply dip your hands in the flour, shake off the excess, and knead. Repeat as necessary. Knead the dough vigorously for 12 minutes.

5. When finished, use a sharp knife to cut the dough into twelve equal parts.

6. Take a section of dough and roll it in your palms to make a ball. Poke your thumbs through the center and work them around to make a hole a bit larger than the size of a quarter. Repeat with remaining eleven sections. Place the formed bagels on a bread-floured work surface about 2 inches apart. Be sure there are no cool drafts directly on them.

7. Cover them with a clean dish towel and let them rise for 25 minutes.

8. Meanwhile, add the remaining 2 tablespoons barley malt syrup to 3 quarts water in a large pot, and bring to a boil. Preheat the oven to 450°. Prepare your cookie sheet or pan by lightly sprinkling it with cornmeal.

9. At the end of 25 minutes, you're ready to place your bagels in the boiling water, four bagels at a time. This stage is called *kettling*. The perfect bagel, when kettled, should quickly sink to the bottom of the pot of boiling water and rise immediately. Boil for about 4 minutes, turning the bagels over frequently with a slotted spoon. If your bagels don't sink to the bottom when you first put them in the pot, don't worry. However, if they sink to the bottom and lie there, wait till they rise to the top (and they will) before timing the 4 minutes.

10. After kettling, remove the bagels from the water with a slotted spoon, allowing any excess water to drain off. Place them close together with edges touching on your cornmeal-prepared cookie sheet or pan.

11. Place pan on rack in middle of oven and bake for 20 minutes. Check bagels by looking at their color; if necessary, continue baking until golden. Watch the bagels carefully toward the end of the baking time because every oven is different and yours may brown quickly. After taking them out of the oven, remove the bagels from the cookie sheet and let them cool on a wire rack for 10 minutes.

Makes 12 bagels

Note: Barley malt syrup is a natural sweetener available at health food stores; if you've refrigerated it, let it come to room temperature before using or microwave it very briefly on low to remove the chill.

CHAPTER 5

Nutritious Low-Fat Recipes to Round Out Your Day

Why did the poppy seed bagel salute the whole-wheat bagel?
Because the whole-wheat bagel is a full kernel.

The road to good nutrition is paved with whole-grain complex carbohydrates, fresh vegetables and fruits, lean and light protein, and no additives or refined sugar. "Real" foods—those in their natural state—nourish and energize the body. You can get back to basics starting with bagel recipes that use natural ingredients.

Tufts University Diet & Nutrition Letter praises the bagel for its high complex carbohydrate content. Depending on the bakery or brand, bagels have little or no fat, and no cholesterol.

The biggest nutritional bang for the bite comes from whole-wheat or other whole-grain bagels. Whole-wheat and whole-grain flours contain practically the entire kernel of grain. A kernel has three basic parts. The outer six layers comprise the *bran.* It contains high percentages of thiamin, riboflavin, niacin, pantothenic acid, protein, and vitamin B_6. The *germ,* at the base of each kernel, contains all of the wheat kernel's vitamin E, protein, and high percentages of riboflavin, thiamin, and B_6. Bran and germ are the sources of the grain's fiber. The majority of the kernel is the *endosperm,* most of which is starch. Though it has much of the kernel's protein and a high percentage of pantothenic acid, endosperm is low in thiamin, B_6, and niacin.

Milling processes that produce refined white flour strip the kernels of nearly all the bran and germ. The remaining endosperm lacks the nutritional value found in whole grains.

Tips for Better Nutrition

Tip 1: Good nutrition is not about deprivation and "dieting." It's about giving your body what it needs to work most efficiently—a variety of real, not synthetic, foods. You feel energized in the process.

Tip 2: Incorporate whole-grain products in your meals whenever you can.

Tip 3: In your quest to lower fat intake, be aware that a product sporting the label "low fat" or "nonfat" is not a green light to gluttony. You may be feeding your body poor imitations of the genuine article with chemicals, additives, sugars, corn syrups, and salt. Besides, excess carbohydrates that aren't used as energy for the body convert to sugar and are stored in the body as fat. Unfortunately, that can put you right back where you started.

Tip 4: Instead of using refined sugars as sweeteners, try natural alternatives. Buy fruit syrups that are all fruit with no added sugar; these are available in health food stores and are recommended for use in all recipes in this chapter calling for fruit syrup. You can also use spoonfuls of frozen pure apple juice concentrate or grated, chopped, or pureed fresh fruit. You'll be delighted with the results.

Tip 5: If you want to eat more healthfully, make changes gradually instead of trying to do it all overnight. Work on one goal at a time. For example, eat more complex carbohydrates and whole grains, avoid high-fat foods, or break your sugar addiction. Incorporate the change into your daily eating habits so that it becomes a way of life. When the first goal is established as a comfortable part of your routine, add another change.

Bagels Roll Over the Competition

	Protein	Carbohydrate	Fat	Sodium	Cholesterol	Calories
Bagel, 2.0 oz	6 gr	30 gr	1.0 gr	320 mg	0 mg	160
Bagel, 4.0 oz.	8 gr	56 gr	1.5 gr	440 mg	0 mg	280
Blueberry Muffin, 4.5 oz	5 gr	59 gr	16 gr	430 mg	0 mg	400
Oat Bran Muffin, 4.5 oz	7 gr	69 gr	8 gr	500 mg	0 mg	370
Corn Muffin, 4.5 oz	6 gr	66 gr	12 gr	690 mg	40 mg	340
Croissant, 2.0 oz	5 gr	25 gr	12 gr	240 mg	35 mg	230
Plain Cake Doughnut, 2.3 oz	4 gr	28 gr	16 gr	260 mg	10 mg	270
Honey-Wheat Glazed Doughnut, 2.8 oz	4 gr	43 gr	17 gr	310 mg	15 mg	340

Gluten Maximus

Bagelberry Slam-Dunk

Enjoy these with a cup of steaming almond extract–flavored coffee.

1 cup nonfat ricotta cheese

One 10-ounce package frozen raspberries, thawed and well-drained

1 cup blueberries (fresh or frozen, thawed and drained)

2 teaspoons raspberry fruit syrup (all fruit, no added sugar)

3 bagels, halved and toasted

In a blender or food processor, blend the ricotta cheese, raspberries, blueberries, and natural raspberry fruit syrup. Cut toasted bagel halves in sections and dunk your way through breakfast.

Makes about 1 1/2 cups (6 servings)

Per serving 1/2 bagel and 1/4 cup dip: 28 g. carbohydrates; 9 g. protein; .25 g. fat; 2 mg. cholesterol; 225 mg. sodium; 183 calories

Strawberries-and-Cream Bagels

3/4 cup fresh strawberries

1/2 cup nonfat ricotta cheese

1 teaspoon strawberry fruit syrup (all fruit, no added sugar)

1 bagel, halved and toasted

Fresh mint (optional)

1. Mash 1/4 cup strawberries and mix with ricotta cheese and strawberry fruit syrup.

2. Blend well and spread each toasted bagel half with mixture.

3. Slice remaining strawberries and place on top of ricotta cheese.

4. Garnish with mint leaves, if desired. Serve open-face.

Makes 2 servings

Per serving: 27 g. carbohydrates; 11 g. protein; .5 g. fat; 2 mg. cholesterol; 225 mg. sodium; 205 calories

Palm Beach Salad Bagels

4 boneless, skinless chicken breasts, cooked and cut into bite-size chunks
  (or a similar amount of turkey breast)
1/3 cup Kraft Free™ Catalina nonfat dressing
1/3 cup nonfat plain yogurt
1/4 cup finely chopped celery
Onion powder, garlic powder, and pepper to taste
1 tablespoon capers (optional)
4 bagels, halved

1. While chicken or turkey chunks are still warm, mix them with dressing; refrigerate for several hours or overnight.

2. Add yogurt and celery, onion powder, garlic powder, salt, and pepper to taste, and capers, if desired. Refrigerate until ready to serve.

3. Make into bagel sandwiches or serve on salad greens with bagels on the side.

Makes 4 servings

Per serving: 49 g. carbohydrates; 46 g. protein; 7 g. fat; 109 mg. cholesterol; 675 mg. sodium; 427 calories

Eggsactly Bagels

8 hard-boiled egg whites, chopped (or microwave egg whites or egg substitute
    till set, then chop)

1 teaspoon Dijon-style mustard

$^1/_4$ cup nonfat yogurt

Dash salt

Pepper to taste

$^1/_4$ cup finely chopped celery or water chestnuts

4 bagels, halved

Mix egg whites, mustard, and yogurt. Add pepper to taste, dash of salt, and celery or water chestnuts. Spread on bagels.

Makes 4 servings

Per serving: 39 g. carbohydrates; 15 g. protein; 0 g. fat; 1.25 mg. cholesterol; 477 mg. sodium; 270 calories

Veggie Bagels

3/4 cup nonfat cottage cheese

1/8 cup very finely chopped radishes

1/8 cup grated green pepper

1/4 cup finely chopped celery

1/8 cup grated carrots

1/4 cup finely chopped scallion

Pepper to taste

1 bagel, halved

Mash cottage cheese with a fork; add radish, green pepper, celery, carrot, scallion, pepper to taste. Spread on bagel halves.

Makes 2 servings

Per serving: 20 g. carbohydrate; 13 g. protein; .5 g. fat; 12 mg. cholesterol; 475 mg. sodium; 169 calories

The Big Dipper

One 16-ounce container nonfat cottage cheese

1 package nonfat powdered Italian dressing

1/2 teaspoon garlic powder

1 tablespoon finely chopped onion

Bagel chips (baked, not fried), carrot sticks, celery sticks, green and red pepper slices

Puree the cottage cheese in a food processor or blender. Fold in the seasonings. Serve with bagel chips and raw veggies for dipping.

Makes about 2 cups (8 servings)

Per 1/4 serving of dip: 3 g. carbohydrates; 8 g. protein; 0 g. fat; 2.5 mg. cholesterol; 85 mg. sodium; 54 calories

Raisin in the Bun

1/2 cup notfat cottage cheese, mashed with a fork

1 teaspoon dark brown sugar

1 tablespoon golden raisins

1 cinnamon-raisin bagel, halved

Blend cottage cheese and brown sugar. Add raisins and mix well. Spread on bagel halves.

Makes 2 servings

Per serving: 29 g. carbohydrates; 11 g. protein; .5 g. fat; 2.5 mg. cholesterol; 115 mg. sodium; 177 calories

Cheese Melts

1 bagel, halved
3 slices fat-free or part-skim mozzarella
2 thin tomato slices
Dash garlic powder
Dash black pepper

Place 1 1/2 slices of cheese on each bagel half. Top each with a slice of tomato. Sprinkle with garlic powder and black pepper. Place in toaster oven or under broiler until cheese melts.

Makes 2 servings

Per serving: 20 g. carbohydrates; 12 g. protein; .53 g. fat; 5 mg. cholesterol; 485 mg. sodium; 138 calories

Bagel Eggels

1/4 cup egg substitute or 2 egg whites
Seasonings to taste
Suggested toppings: your favorite brand of salsa; assorted chopped fresh veggies
*   "sauteed" in water and seasoned to taste*
1 bagel, halved and toasred

Scramble the egg whites or egg substitute according to the package directions. Add seasonings. Spoon onto toasted bagel halves and add the topping of your choice.

Makes 1 serving

Per serving: 30 g. carbohydrates; 13 g. protein; 1 g. fat; 0 mg. cholesterol; 530 mg. sodium; 215 calories

Tuna Trimmer

1 6½-ounce can white tuna in water, drained
2½ tablespoons nonfat plain yogurt
1 tablespoon finely chopped celery
1 teaspoon finely chopped onion (optional)
2 bagels, halved

Mix tuna, yogurt, chopped celery, and onion in a blender or food processor for a couple of seconds, or just until blended. Divide mixture in half to make two bagel sandwiches.

Makes 2 servings

Per serving: 40 g. carbohydrates; 30 g. protein; 3 g. fat; 15 mg. cholesterol; 532 mg. sodium; 314 calories

CHAPTER 6

Breakfast Bagels

Championship golfers would rather eat a bagel than anything else; it always comes with a hole in one.

Strawberry Yogurt Cheese

Use this delicious, nutritious blend as cream cheese. To make it, you'll need some cheesecloth or a paper coffee filter.

1 cup container of nonfat plain yogurt
1/4 cup strawberry fruit syrup (all fruit, no added sugar)

1. Remove lid and any underlid (such as aluminum) from yogurt container.

2. Place cheesecloth or a coffee filter over the yogurt container where the top had been, and secure it with a rubber band.

3. Find a plastic storage container, jar, or bowl just a bit wider than the yogurt container yet deep enough to allow drainage.

4. Quickly turn the container of yogurt upside down, with cheesecloth or filter firmly in place, place it in the "drainage" container, and refrigerate it for at least 48 hours. During this time, the liquid from the yogurt drains out. What remains has a consistency similar to cream cheese.

5. Remove the yogurt cheese from the container and blend in the strawberry fruit syrup. Enjoy it anytime as a bagel spread.

The Big Cheese

2 bagels, halved
4^1/$_2$ ounces brie cheese, cut in thin slices
^{1}/$_3$ cup slivered almonds
Strawberry preserves (all fruit, no added sugar)

1. Preheat the oven to 350°.
2. Cover each bagel half with slices of brie.
3. Top with slivered almonds and bake on a foil-covered cookie sheet until the cheese melts.
4. Serve each half with a small spoonful of strawberry preserves.

Makes 4 halves

Note: For a leaner version, use strawberry yogurt cheese (see pg. 64) instead of brie, and heat for just a few seconds.

Herb Yogurt Cheese

Here's a tasty spiced-up version! Be sure to have on hand a piece of cheesecloth or a paper coffee filter.

> 1 cup container of nonfat plain yogurt
> 1 teaspoon dehydrated minced onion
> 3/8 teaspoon garlic, or more to taste
> 1/8 teaspoon pepper
> 1/8 teaspoon salt
> 2 pinches thyme

1. Remove lid and any underlid (such as aluminum) from yogurt container.

2. Place cheesecloth or coffee filter over the yogurt container where the top had been, and secure it with a rubber band.

3. Find a plastic storage container, jar, or bowl just a bit wider than the yogurt container yet deep enough to allow drainage.

4. Quickly turn the container of yogurt upside down, with cheesecloth or filter firmly in place, place it in the "drainage" container, and refrigerate it for at least 48 hours. During this time, the liquid from the yogurt drains out. What remains has a consistency similar to cream cheese.

5. Remove the yogurt cheese from the container and thoroughly blend in all the spices. Use it anytime as a bagel spread. As a variation, substitute basil and dill for thyme, or experiment to find your personal favorite.

Bagel Castanets

2 eggs, or 4 egg whites, or $^1/_2$ cup egg substitute

Freshly ground pepper to taste

2 tablespoons finely chopped onion or scallion (spring onion)

2 tablespoons finely diced green pepper

1 tablespoon finely chopped black olives

2 tablespoons chopped fresh tomato

1 ounce diced pastrami, corned beef, or turkey pastrami

Nonstick cooking spray or $^1/_2$ teaspoon margarine

1 bagel, halved, toasted, and spread with margarine

Bottled mild taco sauce or salsa, warmed

1. In a bowl, beat the eggs; add 2 tablespoons of water and freshly ground pepper.

2. Add chopped onion, green pepper, olives, tomato, and choice of meat. Mix well.

3. Prepare pan with cooking spray or melt margarine in a frying pan over medium heat; add the egg mixture and scramble until done.

4. Spoon half the mixture onto each bagel half; top with taco sauce or salsa.

   Makes 2 halves

"Oh, what a bagelful morning!"

For-Herring-Lovers-Only Bagels

Bagels, halved
One 8-ounce jar herring in cream sauce or herring marinated in vinegar

Spoon herring and sauce onto toasted bagel halves.

Bagels Benedict

2 bagels, halved
Margarine
4 poached eggs
4 slices Monterey Jack cheese or part-skim mozzarella
Hollandaise Sauce (see Note)
Fresh parsley sprigs for garnish

Toast the bagel halves and spread them with margarine. Top each bagel half with a poached egg. Place a slice of cheese on each egg. Pour on Hollandaise.

Makes 4 halves

Note: To make Hollandaise Sauce: Heat $1/3$ cup margarine until melted and hot. Don't let it brown. Meanwhile, place 2 egg yolks or $1/2$ cup egg substitute, 1 tablespoon lemon juice, and a dash each of white pepper, onion powder, and salt in a blender and blend well. Pour in hot butter or margarine, and blend for a second or two. Makes $3/4$ cup sauce.

Bagel Pancakes

This is a great way to use up stale bagels. For a delightful variation, add grated apple to the batter before frying. You can freeze leftover pancakes and reheat them in a preheated 400° oven for 5 minutes (or if you're in a rush, microwave them for 1 1/2 minutes at full power).

> 3 bagels
>
> 3 eggs, beaten, or 6 egg whites or 3/4 cup egg substitute
>
> 1 1/2 cups low-fat or skim milk
>
> 1/4 plus 1/8 teaspoon salt or onion powder
>
> 3/4 teaspoon sugar or 1 teaspoon frozen apple juice concentrate
>
> 1/3 teaspoon vanilla
>
> Margarine for frying, nonstick cooking spray, or apply small amount of canola oil
> with paper towel
>
> Fruit syrup (all fruit, no added sugar) or small can of fruit in its own juice
> pureed in blender

1. Cut the bagels in small chunks and put in the blender or food processor a few at a time, grinding into crumbs.
2. Place the crumbs in a mixing bowl; add the beaten eggs, milk, salt or onion powder, sugar or juice concentrate, and vanilla. Mix very well. (Mixture will be thick.)
3. Heat the margarine, oil, or cooking spray on a griddle or in a large frying pan.
4. Drop the batter by heaping tablespoons into the pan (as you would regular pancakes). Flatten each with the back of the spoon.
5. Cook slowly over medium heat. You may want to add additional margarine as the pancakes cook to keep the pan from becoming dry. Cook each side until golden-brown.

6. Serve with natural fruit syrup or pureed fruit.

Makes 12 pancakes

Note: If you want to make less than this recipe calls for, one bagel makes four pancakes. Reduce other ingredients accordingly.

Denver Bagels

4 ounces pastrami or bologna or turkey breast, diced
1 tablespoon finely chopped green pepper
1 tablespoon finely chopped onion
Dash pepper
Dash oregano
2 eggs or $1/2$ cup egg substitute, beaten with 2 tablespoons water
1 teaspoon margarine
1 bagel, halved, heated or toasted, and spread lightly with margarine

1. Mix the meat with the green pepper, onion, pepper, and oregano.
2. Add the beaten egg mixture and blend well.
3. Heat the margarine in a frying pan, and scramble the eggs until firm.
4. Spoon the mixture onto the bagel halves. Serve open-faced.

Makes 2 halves

Scrambled Bagel

1 bagel

1 egg, 2 egg whites, or $1/4$ cup egg substitute

2 tablespoons cream cheese, cut in small pieces, or Herb Yogurt Cheese (see page 66)

1 tablespoon low-fat or skim milk

Freshly ground pepper to taste

Salt to taste

$1/2$ teaspoon chopped scallion or chives (optional)

Nonstick cooking spray or canola oil

1. Slice off the top quarter of the bagel horizontally. (See drawing on page 82.) Set the "top" aside.
2. Carefully scoop out the inside of the remaining bagel with your fingers and set aside the bagel bits, leaving a bagel "shell."
3. Heat the bagel shell and top in the oven; while they are warming, beat the egg or egg substitute with a fork or whisk.
4. Finely crumble the bagel bits you scooped out; add the crumbs to the egg.
5. Add the cream cheese or yogurt cheese, milk, pepper, salt, and scallion, if desired.
6. Prepare frying pan with a light coating of spray or oil; scramble the egg until dry.
7. Fill the warmed bagel shell with cooked egg, and replace the bagel top.

Makes 1 serving

Note: For variety, experiment by adding shredded part-skim mozzarella cheese and/or sliced cooked mushrooms to the egg mixture before cooking.

Bullseye Bagels

I bagel, halved
I teaspoon margarine
Cooking spray or canola oil
2 slices bologna or smoked turkey breast
2 eggs, 4 egg whites, or $^1/_2$ cup egg substitute
Freshly ground pepper

1. Toast the bagel halves lightly and spread each with $^1/_2$ teaspoon margarine. Prepare a frying pan with cooking spray or wipe with canola oil.

2. Meanwhile, heat the bologna or turkey slices on both sides in the pan; place one slice on each toasted bagel half.

3. Fry the eggs until set.

4. Sprinkle the eggs with freshly ground pepper and place one on each bagel half. Serve open-faced.

Makes 2 halves

Sunrise Bagel

1 bagel, halved
1 turkey-sausage patty, cooked

Heat or toast the bagel halves in a toaster oven. Add the sausage to make a bagel sandwich.

Makes 1 serving.

Bagels by the Sea

1 bagel, halved
Herb Yogurt Cheese (see pg. 66)
4 ounces smoked whitefish or 2 slices sable (from your favorite deli) or
    mix 1 can water-packed salmon, drained, with 2 teaspoons nonfat plain yogurt
4 cucumber slices
4 thin onion slices
Fresh spinach or Boston lettuce leaf

Spread bottom bagel half with a coating of Herb Yogurt Cheese. Place fish on top. Top with cucumber and onion slices. Cover with spinach or Boston lettuce leaf and other bagel half.

Makes 1 serving

The Traditional Bagel

1 bagel, halved

1 tablespoon nonfat cream cheese or Herb Yogurt Cheese (see pg. 66)

2 good-size slices smoked salmon

2 thick tomato slices

2 thin onion slices (optional)

Spread the bagel halves with cream cheese. Top each with a slice of smoked salmon, tomato, and onion, if desired. Serve open-face or (for the adventurous) as a big sandwich.

Makes 2 halves or 1 bagel sandwich

CHAPTER 7

Luncheon and Dinner Bagels

Bagel deli owners make the best jailers because
they always have lox.

Bagelcues

2 bagels, halved
1 pound lean ground beef, turkey, or chicken
1/4 teaspoon garlic powder
1 onion, finely chopped
1 tablespoon dark brown sugar
1/2 cup barbecue sauce (any kind)

1. Preheat the oven to 375°.

2. With your fingers, scoop out the insides of the bagel halves, leaving "shells." Place the scooped-out bits in a blender and process to make fine crumbs.

3. In a frying pan over medium heat, crumble the ground meat; add the garlic powder and chopped onion, and cook thoroughly. Drain off fat.

4. Add the brown sugar, bagel crumbs, and barbecue sauce, and stir well over low heat.

5. Fill the bagel shells with the meat mixture, and bake on a foil-covered cookie sheet in the preheated oven for about 15 minutes, or until heated thoroughly.

Makes 4 halves

Deli Boss Bagel

1 bagel, halved
Mustard
2 ounces turkey pastrami
1 ounce lean roast beef
2 tablespoons chopped liver

Spread one bagel half with a thin coat of mustard. Place the pastrami and roast beef on top of the mustard. Spread chopped liver on other bagel half and make a great deli sandwich.

Makes 1 serving

Bagels Bourguignonne

1 cup flour

1 teaspoon seasoned salt or non-salt seasoning substitute

2 pounds pot roast, cut into bite-size cubes (or use stew beef chunks or
    chicken breast chunks)

1 tablespoon olive oil

1 cup beef consommé (use chicken consommé if cooking with chicken)

1/2 cup dry white wine

1 minced garlic clove

1 finely chopped onion

2 carrots, peeled and julienned

2 finely chopped celery stalks

4 bagels, halved

1. Mix the flour and seasoning and put in a plastic bag. Add the beef or chicken cubes and toss thoroughly to coat with flour mixture.

2. Heat the oil in a large heavy pot and brown the meat thoroughly.

3. Pour the consommé and wine over the meat.

4. Add the garlic, onion, carrot, and celery. Stir well.

5. Bring to a boil; reduce heat and let simmer for 2 to 3 hours, stirring periodically.

6. Serve over hot bagel halves.

Makes 4 servings

Bagel Burger

1 bagel, halved
1/4 pound ground beef, turkey, or chicken patty
1/4 onion, chopped or sliced
Nonstick cooking spray or canola oil
Shredded lettuce
Bottled Thousand Island fat-free salad dressing or mild or spicy salsa

1. Heat or toast the bagel, or use it plain.

2. Prepare pan by spraying it with nonstick cooking spray or wiping it lightly with canola oil. Fry meat patty in the onion, and place it on one half of the bagel.

3. Top with shredded lettuce, salad dressing or salsa, and other bagel half. Then get ready to open wide!

Makes 1 serving

Bagels and Gravy

Leftover gravy from roast or bottled "homestyle" gravy (see Note)
Bagels, halved

Heat the gravy in a saucepan. Spoon over heated or toasted bagel halves.

Note: Make your own gravy, or choose whatever flavor bottled gravy you prefer; there are nonfat varieties available. Brown gravy, chicken gravy, mushroom gravy, turkey gravy, and onion gravy are all great on bagels! You can also sauté chopped fresh mushrooms and onions in natural skimmed turkey or chicken juices.

Bagel Tuna Boats

4 bagels
One 6$1/2$-ounce can white tuna packed in water, drained
One 10$1/2$-ounce can low-fat cream of mushroom soup
2 tablespoons fresh parsley, chopped
$1/2$ of an 8-ounce can water chestnuts, rinsed, drained, and chopped
$1/2$ tablespoon olive oil or canola oil

1. Preheat the oven to 375°.

2. With a serrated knife, slice a thin portion off the top of each bagel. Using your fingers, scoop out the insides of the bagels and reserve, leaving bagel "boats." Set aside.

3. Put the drained tuna in a mixing bowl and separate into fine pieces with your fingers.

4. Fold in the undiluted can of cream of mushroom soup, parsley, and water chestnuts, and mix until well blended.

5. Fill each bagel boat with a little less than a $1/2$ cup of tuna mixture.

6. Crumble some of the scooped-out bagel bits with your fingers (or in a blender or food processor) to make fine crumbs.

7. Heat oil in a frying pan; add the crumbs and stir quickly, until they are light brown.

8. Sprinkle the crumbs over the tuna mixture in the bagels. Bake on a foil-covered cooking sheet for 15 to 20 minutes, or until thoroughly heated.

Makes 4 servings

Note: You can put the bagel tops and any bagel bits you didn't use for crumbs into a plastic bag and freeze for later use. You can also freeze the filled tuna boats and reheat them in a preheated 400° oven for 10 minutes.

Soup and Bagels

For a satisfying and fun meal, make a tureenful of your favorite hearty soup. Serve with a big basket of assorted hot, toasty, lightly buttered bagels.

Bagel Stuffing

A great way to use up stale bagels!

> 3 bagels, cut into small cubes
>
> 1/4 cup margarine
>
> 1 celery stalk, chopped
>
> 1 medium onion, chopped
>
> 8 mushrooms, chopped
>
> 1/8 cup chopped fresh parsley
>
> 1/4 teaspoon poultry seasoning (use salt-free if desired)
>
> 2 eggs, 1/2 cup egg substitute, or 4 egg whites, beaten

1. Put the bagel cubes on a foil-covered cookie sheet and bake in a preheated 375° oven for 15 minutes. Place the cubes in a mixing bowl.

2. In a large frying pan, melt margarine; sauté celery, onion, mushroom, and parsley until tender.

3. Stir in the poultry seasoning and mix thoroughly.

4. Pour the mixture over the bagel cubes in the bowl and mix well.

5. Add the eggs or egg substitute and mix thoroughly. Refrigerate the stuffing mixture until chilled before stuffing poultry.

Enough stuffing for 8 pounds of poultry.

Note: To stuff a 4-pound chicken, simply cut the recipe in half. Or if you'd rather stuff yourself than the chicken, add bite-size chunks of cooked poultry to the stuffing mixture, bake in a lightly greased casserole dish for 1 hour at 375°, and enjoy as a main course.

The art of being well-bread

Beef-o-Bagels

4 bagels, halved

1 tablespoon soft margarine

1 1/2 tablespoons mustard

1 pound very lean ground beef, turkey, or chicken

1/4 cup regular or fruit-sweetened catsup, marinara sauce, or salsa

1 onion (small or medium), chopped fine

1/4 teaspoon garlic powder

1/4 teaspoon seasoned salt or salt substitute

1. Place the bagel halves under the broiler until cut sides are toasted.

2. Meanwhile, blend the margarine and mustard.

3. Remove the bagel halves from the broiler, and spread the cut sides completely to the edges with margarine-mustard mixture. (You'll use half of the mixture for this, and the rest at the end of the recipe.)

4. In a bowl, place the meat, catsup, onion, garlic powder, and seasoned salt; mix well with your hands.

5. Divide the mixture into four portions. Take one portion, divide it in half again, and press it onto a bagel half, spreading it all the way to the edges. Repeat with the remaining bagel halves.

6. Place them under the broiler for 10 to 12 minutes, or until the meat is cooked.

7. Remove form the broiler and immediately spread the top of each with remaining margarine-mustard mixture.

Makes 8 halves

Whopper Bagel

1 bagel, halved

4 ounces corned beef (heated or cold), turkey breast, or smoked turkey breast

1/4 cup coleslaw

1 teaspoon regular or fruit-sweetened catsup

1 tablespoon regular or nonfat mayonnaise

Place the corned beef on one bagel half; top with coleslaw. Mix the catsup and mayonnaise; spread on other bagel half and place on top. This recipe makes one whopper of a bagel! (If you prefer, you can serve it open-faced on two halves.)

Makes 1 serving

Iron Bagel

1 bagel, halved

1 teaspoon nonfat mayonnaise

    or 1/2 teaspoon nonfat yogurt mixed with 1/2 teaspoon mustard

1/2 cup chopped liver

1 slice tomato

1 large spinach leaf

Spread each bagel half with 1/2 teaspoon of mayonnaise or yogurt-mustard. Top with chopped liver and tomato slices, and spinach leaf, and make a bagel sandwich.

Makes 1 serving

Bagel Garlic Bread

4 bagels, halved

Olive oil

Garlic powder

Oregano

Grated reduced-fat or nonfat Parmesan or part-skim mozzarella cheese

1. Preheat the oven to 375°.

2. Drizzle each bagel half with olive oil.

3. Generously sprinkle with garlic powder, oregano, and Parmesan or mozzarella.

4. Cut each half in half again vertically.

5. Place on a foil-covered cooking sheet; bake until the bagels are thoroughly heated and the tops start to brown.

Makes 16 pieces

Poorboy Bagel

1 bagel, halved

2 teaspoons mustard

2 slices turkey salami or turkey bologna

1 spinach leaf

2 thin tomato slices

Spread the bagel halves with mustard. Place the salami or turkey bologna slices on one half; top with spinach leaf, tomato slices, and other bagel half.

Makes 1 serving

Bagel Melts

One 6 1/2-ounce can white tuna packed in water, well drained and flaked

3 tablespoons nonfat mayonnaise or

      2 tablespoons nonfat plain yogurt and 1 tablespoon mustard

1 tomato, cut into cubes

1 celery stalk, chopped

2 bagels, halved

4 slices nonfat cheddar cheese or part-skim mozzarella

1. Preheat the broiler.

2. Mix the tuna, mayonnaise or yogurt-mustard, tomato cubes, and celery until well blended. Spoon onto bagel halves. Top each half with a slice of cheese.

3. Place under the broiler, and cook until the cheese melts.

Makes 4 halves

Chili Bagels

2 bagels, halved

One 15-ounce can chili, or nonfat vegetarian spicy chili with black beans

1 small onion, finely chopped

1 medium tomato, chopped

1. Toast the bagel halves or heat them in the oven.

2. Meanwhile, heat the chili in a saucepan.

3. Spoon the chili onto the heated bagel halves; top with chopped onion and tomato.

Makes 4 halves

Bagel Croutons

Here's another good recipe for using up stale bagels.

$1/3$ cup extra-virgin olive oil

1 garlic clove, thinly sliced

3 bagels, cut into cubes

$1/2$ cup grated reduced-fat or nonfat Parmesan

$1/8$ cup dried parsley

1. Place the oil and garlic in a small bowl; let sit for 1 hour.
2. Heat the garlic oil in a large frying pan; add the bagel cubes and cook until crisp and golden-brown, tossing constantly.
3. Drain on paper towels.
4. When cool, toss the croutons with Parmesan and parsley, and add them to your favorite salad.

Makes approximately 2 cups

Club Bagel

1 bagel, cut in thirds horizontally, as shown

*Nonfat Thousand Island salad dressing, or use extra-virgin olive oil and
    balsamic vinegar in equal amounts*
1 slice corned beef
1/8 cup chopped liver
2 slices (2 ounces) turkey or chicken
2 Boston lettuce or spinach leaves
2 slices tomato

Spread salad dressing on each layer of bagel, or drizzle oil and vinegar combination. Place corned beef and chopped liver on one bagel layer. Top with a second bagel layer and add turkey, lettuce, and tomato. Cover with remaining third of bagel.

Makes 1 serving

Sloppy Bagels

1 pound lean ground beef, turkey, or chicken

1 celery stalk, finely chopped

1 medium onion, finely chopped

3/4 teaspoon salt or seasoning substitute

1/8 teaspoon pepper

16 ounces bottled or canned spaghetti sauce

1/4 pound mushrooms, sliced thin

3 bagels, halved

1. Brown the meat in a large frying pan with the celery, onion, salt, and pepper. Drain off any fat.

2. Add the spaghetti sauce and mushrooms to the meat.

3. Simmer, uncovered, over low heat for about 10 minutes, stirring occasionally.

4. Toast the bagel halves in a toaster or oven. Spoon the mixture onto the bagel halves and serve.

Makes 6 halves

The Wurst Bagel

1 jumbo cooked hot dog or knockwurst, or use turkey or chicken "dog"

1 bagel, halved

1/4 cup sauerkraut, rinsed and well drained

1 teaspoon India relish (optional)

Mustard and/or catsup

Slice the hot dog in half and then into thin strips; place the strips on one bagel half. Top with sauerkraut; add relish, if desired. Spread mustard and/or catsup on the other bagel half and place on top.

Makes 1 serving

Bagel Chicken Mignon

2 teaspoons extra-virgin olive oil

2 boneless, skinless chicken breasts, pounded thin

1 small onion, thinly sliced

4 mushrooms, thinly sliced

1/4 green pepper, thinly sliced

1 bagel, halved

Garlic powder, freshly ground pepper, or sage to taste

1. Heat the oil in frying pan. Lightly brown chicken on both sides. Lower heat.
2. Add the onion, mushroom, and green pepper slices, and seasonings to taste. Cook until chicken is done. If liquid evaporates while cooking, add a little bit of water to prevent pan from drying out. Spoon the mixture onto the bagel halves.

Makes 2 halves

Stir-Fried Bagels

Make your favorite recipe for vegetarian stir-fry, spoon over toasted bagel halves, top with cheese, and broil until the cheese has melted. (You can also use chicken or beef stir-fry and omit the cheese.) Delicious!

CHAPTER 8

Vegetarian Bagels

*These days everybody's a bagel expert. Even the jeweler
down the street invented a two-carrot bagel.*

Bagel Bruschetta

4 medium-size ripe tomatoes, preferably plum tomatoes, chopped

1 1/2 tablespoons minced fresh garlic

1/8 cup chopped fresh basil

1/4 cup chopped cilantro

1 1/2 teaspoons lemon juice

Freshly ground pepper and salt to taste

2 bagels, halved

4 teaspoons extra-virgin olive oil

1. Thoroughly combine first six ingredients and refrigerate for several hours or overnight. When ready to serve, bring to room temperature.

2. Brush cut sides of bagels with olive oil and toast lightly in toaster oven. Spoon tomato mixture onto bagel halves and serve open-face.

Makes 4 servings

Veggie Bagel Burger

1 bagel, halved
1 ground vegetable patty, cooked according to package directions
2 thin onion slices
2 spinach leaves
Nonfat or low-fat salad dressing, or nonfat plain yogurt mixed with freshly ground pepper and regular or fruit-sweetened catsup (available at health food stores) to taste

1. Place cooked vegetable patty on bagel half. Add onion slices, spinach leaves, and spoonful of dressing.

2. Top with other bagel half.

Makes 1 bagel sandwich

Health Bagel

1 bagel, halved
2 teaspoons mayonnaise or Herb Yogurt Cheese (see pg. 66) or unseasoned Yogurt Cheese mixed with 1/2 teaspoon mustard or salsa
1 small avocado, peeled and sliced
2 tablespoons alfalfa sprouts
1/2 cup shredded Monterey Jack cheese
1 tablespoon sesame chips, crumbled

Spread the bagel halves lightly with mayonnaise or yogurt cheese. Place the avocado slices, then alfalfa sprouts on each half. Put 1/4 cup of cheese on each, and top with sesame chips.

Makes 2 halves

Bagel Soufflé

This is an absolutely scrumptious main dish or side dish! Every bite is heavenly.

  1 tablespoon margarine
  Nonstick cooking spray
  4 bagels, halved
  7 eggs or 1¾ cups egg substitute
  ¼ teaspoon salt
  2 cups low-fat or skim milk
  ¼ teaspoon paprika
  Freshly ground pepper
  6 ounces regular, low-fat, or nonfat Monterey Jack cheese, grated
  6 ounces regular, low-fat, or nonfat cheddar cheese, grated

1. Grease a 2-quart casserole with tablespoon of margarine or butter, followed by a light coating of cooking spray. Cut the bagel halves into small bite-size pieces and set aside.

2. In a mixing bowl, beat together the eggs, salt, milk, paprika, and pepper.

3. Place half of the bagel cubes in the greased casserole. Mix the cheeses together; place half of the cheese mixture on top of the bagel cubes; repeat with the remaining bagel cubes and remaining cheese.

4. Carefully ladle the egg mixture into the casserole dish on top of the bagel-cheese layers, making sure to cover evenly so it seeps through. (You may want to poke holes through with a knife as you ladle.)

5. Set the casserole in the refrigerator and let it stand overnight, or until you are ready to bake it the next day.

6. Preheat the oven to 350°.

7. Bake the casserole in preheated oven for 1 hour, or until top is golden.

  Makes 8 servings

Hummus Bagels

One 16-ounce can chick peas (garbanzo beans), rinsed and drained
1/2 cup store-bought tahini sauce (sesame-seed dressing) or 1/4 cup sesame oil
    with 1/4 cup balsamic vinegar
2 bagels, halved
Garlic powder to taste
Alfalfa sprouts

1. Place the chick peas in a blender or food processor, and blend until smooth.

2. Add the tahini sauce or sesame oil and vinegar; blend until completely mixed.

3. Add garlic powder to taste. You've just made hummus!

4. Put heaping 1/4 cup of hummus on each bagel half and top with alfalfa sprouts. Or you can simply put a bowl of hummus on the table, surrounded with bagel chunks or bagel chips as well as cut-up fresh vegetables for dipping.

   Makes 4 halves

Mushroom Bagels

1 cup chopped fresh mushrooms
1 small onion, chopped
2 teaspoons extra-virgin olive oil
1/4 teaspoon dried thyme
Dash salt
1 bagel, halved
2 slices Swiss, Muenster, low-fat Swiss, or part-skim mozzarella cheese

1. Preheat the oven to 375°.
2. Saute the mushrooms and onion in olive oil; stir in the thyme and salt.
3. Spoon the mixture on the bagel halves; top each with a slice of cheese.
4. Bake on a foil-covered cookie sheet for 8 to 10 minutes, or until the cheese melts.

Makes 2 halves

The Winner's Circle

1 bagel, halved
2 teaspoons regular or nonfat mayonnaise
2 hard-boiled eggs or egg whites, sliced
1 Boston lettuce leaf
Herbs and freshly ground pepper to taste
Dash salt

Spread the mayonnaise on the bagel halves. Place the hard-boiled egg slices on one half, then a lettuce leaf. Sprinkle with herbs, pepper, and salt to taste. Add other bagel half.

Makes 1 serving

Eggsotic Bagels

8 hard-boiled egg whites, chopped

1/3 cup chopped salt-free dry-roasted peanuts or unsalted walnuts

1/2 cup nonfat plain yogurt mixed with 2 tablespoons mustard

Salt to taste

4 bagels, halved

Combine the chopped eggs or egg whites, nuts, yogurt-mustard, and salt to taste. Spoon onto four bagel halves; top with remaining halves to make sandwiches.

Makes 4 servings

Kojak Bagel

1 bagel, halved

Olive oil

Shredded lettuce

4 ounces feta cheese, crumbled

2 thin onion slices

2 tomato slices

4 pitted Greek olives, sliced (or cucumber slices)

2 slices of anchovies or sweet red pepper slices

Drizzle the bagel halves very lightly with olive oil. Place a small amount of shredded lettuce on each. Add feta cheese, onion, and tomato slices; top with sliced olives or cucumbers and anchovies and pepper slices, if desired.

Makes 2 halves

Tofu Bagel

10 ounces tofu

1/4 cup nonfat mayonnaise or extra-virgin olive oil and vinegar dressing

2 teaspoons Dijon-style mustard

1/2 teaspoon garlic powder

3/4 cup finely chopped celery

3/4 cup finely chopped green pepper

1 small onion, finely chopped

1 tablespoon Tamari sauce or balsamic vinegar

2 bagels, halved

Drain and mash the tofu. Mix it with the remaining ingredients, except the bagels, and blend well. Spoon one-fourth of the mixture onto each bagel half.

Makes 4 halves

Cheese Toppers

Whole bagels

Slices of your favorite cheese

Top whole bagels with slices of your favorite cheese. Place in oven or toaster oven and heat thoroughly until cheese melts.

Easy-Cheesy Bagels

1 bagel, halved

2 tablespoons cream cheese, nonfat cream cheese, or Herb Yogurt Cheese (see pg. 66)

1 ounce low-fat or nonfat cheddar cheese, shredded

1 ounce Monterey Jack cheese or part-skim mozzarella, shredded

4 stuffed green olives, sliced

Spread each bagel half with a tablespoon of cream cheese or yogurt cheese. Mix shredded cheeses together and spoon onto halves. Top with olive slices.

Makes 2 halves

California Bagel Spread

One 4-ounce package cream cheese or nonfat cream cheese or 1/2 cup unseasoned Yogurt Cheese (see pg. 64)

1 1/2 tablespoons honey, apricot fruit syrup (all fruit, no added sugar), or frozen apple juice concentrate

1/8 cup golden raisins

1 medium carrot, peeled and grated

1/4 cup chopped walnuts

Bagels, halved

Mix the cream cheese and honey or apricot fruit syrup or apple juice concentrate with an electric mixer or food processor. Stir in the raisins, carrot, and walnuts by hand. Spread on bagels.

Makes approximately 1 cup of spread

Sir Bagel Olive-ier

1 bagel, halved
Nonfat cream cheese or Herb Yogurt Cheese (see pg. 66)
Stuffed green olives, sliced
Finely chopped walnuts

Spread the bagel halves generously with cream cheese or yogurt cheese. Top with stuffed green olive slices and sprinkle with walnuts.

Makes 2 halves

Delhi Bagels

If you like curry, you'll love this!

1/2 cup soft or whipped low-fat or nonfat cream cheese
1/4 teaspoon plus 1/8 teaspoon curry powder
2 teaspoons chutney
1/8 cup finely chopped unsalted dry-roasted peanuts or unsalted walnuts
1 tablespoon shredded sweetened coconut
1 bagel, halved

Mix the cream cheese or yogurt cheese, curry powder, chutney, nuts, and coconut; blend well. Spread on bagel halves.

Makes 2 halves

Bagel Beer Fondue

I small garlic clove, halved

3/4 cup beer

I tablespoon flour

8 ounces Swiss cheese or part-skim mozzarella, shredded

4 ounces sharp cheddar cheese, shredded (can substitute low-fat or nonfat)

Freshly ground pepper

1/8 teaspoon paprika

5 bagels, cut in large bite-size chunks

1. Rub the inside of a heavy saucepan with the garlic; discard the garlic.
2. Add the beer and heat slowly.
3. Meanwhile, place the flour in a plastic bag; add the shredded cheese and shake to coat.
4. Gradually add the flour-cheese mixture to the beer. Stir constantly until thickened and bubbly, but do not boil.
5. Stir in the pepper and paprika.
6. Pour the mixture into a fondue pot, and serve with bagel chunks. (Spear chunks and dip into hot cheese mixture to coat. Add more warmed beer if the fondue becomes too thick.)

   Makes approximately 2 1/4 cups

Swiss Bagels

1/8 cup regular or nonfat mayonnaise
1 cup diced Swiss cheese or part-skim mozzarella
1 teaspoon dried or 1 tablespoon freshly chopped parsley
2 bagels, halved
4 slices dill pickle (optional)

1. Preheat the oven to 375°.

2. Mix the mayonnaise, cheese, and parsley.

3. Spoon the mixture onto the bagel halves, and bake on a foil-covered cookie sheet for about 10 minutes, or until the cheese melts. Top each half with a dill pickle slice, if desired, before serving.

Makes 4 halves

Blue Bagels

1/2 cup regular or nonfat mayonnaise
1 tablespoon dried or fresh chopped parsley
1 cup crumbled blue cheese
2 bagels, halved
4 tomato slices

1. Preheat the broiler.

2. Mix the mayonnaise, parsley, and cheese. Spread onto bagel halves.

3. Place under the broiler until the cheese has melted.

4. Remove, and top each half with a tomato slice.

Makes 4 halves

Mexicali Bagel Fondue

3 bagels, halved

1 small onion, finely chopped

1/3 cup extra-virgin olive oil

One 4-ounce can mild chopped green chilies

Flour

One 15-ounce can whole tomatoes, mashed (do not drain)

Worcestershire or Tamari sauce to taste

Garlic powder to taste

12 ounces shredded nonfat cheddar cheese, or part-skim mozzarella

1. Toast the bagel halves in a toaster or oven.

2. Cut each half into ten "chunks"; set aside.

3. In a frying pan, brown the onion in olive oil; add the chilies.

4. Add enough flour to make a thick paste.

5. Over low heat add the tomatoes, Worcestershire or Tamari sauce, and garlic powder; mix well.

6. Stir in the cheese, and blend all of the ingredients together over low heat.

7. Serve in a fondue pot. Spear toasted bagel chunks and dip into hot cheese mixture to coat.

Makes approximately 3 1/2 cups

Bagels Parmesan

1 cup grated regular, reduced fat, or nonfat Parmesan

1/4 cup regular or nonfat mayonnaise

1 medium onion, grated

2 bagels, halved

Paprika

1. Preheat the oven to 375°.

2. Mix the cheese with the mayonnaise and onion; blend well.

3. Spread onto bagel halves; sprinkle each with a dash of paprika.

4. Bake for 10 minutes, or until golden.

Makes 4 halves

CHAPTER 9

Bagel Party Fare

Some uninformed people think bagels
are doughnuts with arthritis.

Bagels Italiano

Bagels, halved
Bottled oil and vinegar salad dressing
Grated Parmesan
Oregano
Dash garlic powder

1. Preheat the oven to 375°.

2. Cut each bagel half in four sections and place on a foil-covered cookie sheet.

3. Carefully spoon 1 teaspoon of dressing on top of each section.

4. Sprinkle with Parmesan, oregano, and garlic powder.

5. Place the cookie sheet in the oven, and bake for 10 minutes, or until golden.

Rumaki Bagels

1 pound chicken livers, drained

1 small onion, chopped

2 tablespoons bottled Tamari sauce

One 20-ounce can pineapple chunks in own juice, drained; reserve juice

One 8-ounce can water chestnuts, drained, rinsed, and chopped

3 bagels, halved

Fresh parsley for garnish

1. In a frying pan, cook the chicken livers with onion, Tamari sauce and $1/4$ cup reserved pineapple juice. As the livers cook, cut them into small pieces with a knife and fork.

2. When the livers are completely cooked, remove the pan from the heat; add the water chestnuts.

3. Blend in food processor for 2 to 3 seconds.

4. Spoon onto bagel halves. Cut each half in quarters. Garnish with fresh parsley, and refrigerate until serving time. You can also serve these warm: Just heat them for 10 minutes in a 375° oven. This recipe freezes beautifully. Serve with colorful toothpick-speared pineapple chunks on the side.

Makes 24 portions

Fish and Chips

¹/2 pound fish fillet (any kind), cooked

¹/4 cup nonfat yogurt

1 celery stalk, chopped fine

¹/2 teaspoon Spike™ seasoning

1 teaspoon dehydrated onion flakes or 1 tablespoon fresh chopped onion

Ground pepper to taste

One 6-ounce bag bagel chips

Crumble the fish in a mixing bowl with a fork. Add the yogurt and mix well. Add the chopped celery, seasoning, onion, and pepper, and mix until well blended. Serve as a dip with bagel chips. This is also good spooned on bagel halves, or atop shredded lettuce with a toasted bagel on the side.

Makes approximately 2 cups

Ring Around the Bagel

4 onion bagels, halved

8 ounces cream cheese or 1 cup Herb Yogurt Cheese (see pg. 66)

4 hard-boiled eggs, finely chopped

1 small onion, finely chopped

One 1-ounce jar caviar

1. Spread each bagel half with approximately ¹/8 cup (2 tablespoons) of cheese, spreading completely to the edges and covering the bagel hole.

2. Using a small spoon, carefully place the chopped egg on the cream cheese, forming a circle along the outside edge of the bagel halves. Press the egg gently into the cream cheese. When you've finished, each one will look like it has a "wreath" of chopped egg.

3. Make a circle of chopped onion inside the circle of chopped egg.

4. Place a spoonful of caviar in the center of each bagel half.

Makes 8 halves

Note: For an alternative to caviar, try flaked canned tuna or salmon.

Sardinia Bagels

One 8-ounce package cream cheese, softened
One 3.7-ounce tin sardines, rinsed and well drained
1/4 cup finely minced onion
6 bagels, halved

In a small bowl, mash the sardines. Add the cream cheese and blend well. Stir in the minced onion. Serve as a spread with bagels.

Makes approximately 1 3/4 cups

Bagel Coins

¹/2 cup extra-virgin olive oil

1 to 2 garlic cloves, minced (use a garlic press if you have one)

3 bagels, sliced into thin "coins" as shown, using serrated knife

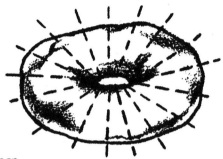

¹/4 cup grated Parmesan

¹/2 cup dry-roasted peanuts

1. Place the oil in a large frying pan; add the minced garlic, and stir well. (For onion-flavored coins, substitute dehydrated onion flakes for the garlic cloves.)

2. Heat the oil and add the bagel "coins." Fry until brown and crisp on both sides.

3. Drain on paper towels. When cool, place in a plastic bag with the Parmesan, and toss well.

4. Remove from the bag, mix with the peanuts, and serve. Bagel coins store well in a tightly capped jar.

Makes approximately 2 ¹/2 cups

White Pizza Bagels

4 bagels, halved
Extra-virgin olive oil
Garlic powder
8 ounces fontina cheese
8 ounces grated Parmesan

1. Preheat the oven to 375°.

2. Brush each bagel half with olive oil. Sprinkle with a dash of garlic powder.

3. Top each half with 1 ounce of fontina and sprinkle each with 1 teaspoon Parmesan. Bake for 8 to 10 minutes, or until cheese is melted and top is lightly browned.

Makes 8 servings

CHAPTER 10

For Your Sweet Tooth

What do you get when you combine bagels, religion, and outer space?
Holey UFOs.

Bagel Cheese Pastries

These are heavenly! If you'd like, you can make these a day ahead or freeze them (and thaw at room temperature before serving).

4 cinnamon-raisin bagels, halved

One 8-ounce package nonfat cream cheese, softened (bring to room temperature)

1/4 cup granulated sugar

1/8 teaspoon ground cinnamon

2 teaspoons lemon juice

1 egg or 1/4 cup egg substitute

1 teaspoon vanilla extract

One 20-ounce can cherry pie filling, or use fresh fruit

1. Preheat the oven to 375°.

2. With your fingers, scoop out some of the insides of the bagel halves to make shells. Freeze the scooped-out bits for other uses (such as bread crumbs or poultry stuffing).

3. In a mixing bowl, combine the cream cheese, sugar, cinnamon, lemon juice, egg, and vanilla. Beat well with an electric mixer, until the ingredients are thoroughly blended.

4. Carefully spoon the mixture into the bagel shells.

5. Bake on a foil-covered cookie sheet for 15 minutes, or until filling sets.

6. When cool, top each half with a couple of spoonfuls of cherry pie filling, or better yet, use slices of your favorite fresh fruit—kiwi, strawberries, peaches, blueberries. They taste delicious and make a festive presentation.

Makes 8 halves

Butterscotch Bagels

2 bagels, halved

2 teaspoons margarine

1 cup butterscotch chips

One 2 1/4-ounce package chopped unsalted walnuts

1. Preheat the oven to 375°.

2. Spread each bagel half with 1/2 teaspoon of margarine, and place on a foil-covered cookie sheet.

3. Top each half with 1/4 cup of butterscotch chips.

4. Top with chopped walnuts, and bake for 15 to 20 minutes, or until the chips melt.

Makes 4 halves

Perfectly Pecan Bagels

3 cinnamon-raisin bagels, halved

3 eggs or $3/4$ cup egg substitute

$1/2$ cup dark brown sugar

$1/2$ cup light corn syrup

$1/8$ teaspoon salt

1 teaspoon vanilla extract

1 teaspoon margarine, melted

$3/4$ cup chopped pecans

30 pecan halves for garnish

1. Preheat the oven to 375°.

2. Scoop out the insides of the bagel halves with your fingers. Crumble the scooped-out bits, and set them aside. You will have six "shells."

3. In a mixing bowl, beat the eggs; add the brown sugar, corn syrup, salt, and vanilla. Beat well.

4. Add the melted margarine and blend.

5. Stir in the chopped pecans and crumbled bagel bits; mix thoroughly.

6. Spoon the mixture carefully into the bagel halves, and top each with five pecan halves.

7. Bake on a foil-covered cookie sheet for approximately 25 minutes, or until lightly browned.

8. Transfer to a plate to cool, or they will stick to the foil.

Makes 6 halves

Chocolate-Covered Bagel Chips

12 ounces semisweet chocolate chips

3 tablespoons canola oil

One 6-ounce bag plain bagel chips (don't buy flavored chips such as garlic, onion, etc.)

1/2 cup chopped walnuts

1/2 cup shredded sweetened coconut

1. Place the chocolate chips and oil in a saucepan. Over low heat, stir constantly with a wooden spoon until the chips melt and the mixture is blended thoroughly.

2. Keeping the saucepan on a very low flame, drop the bagel chips in the chocolate one at a time, turning to coat. Use a wooden spoon to make sure both sides are thoroughly coated. Spoon off the excess chocolate, and place them on a wax paper–covered cookie sheet.

3. When all of the bagel chips are coated and on wax paper, sprinkle some with coconut and some with chopped nuts. Refrigerate until the chocolate hardens. If you've used whole bagel chips, you can break them into small pieces if you'd like.

Makes enough to coat 14 whole bagel chips.

Note: Be sure to keep these in the refrigerator until serving time. (It's also a good place to hide them from chocoholics.) True chocolate lovers can use chocolate sprinkles in place of coconut and nuts. Rainbow sprinkles are fun, too!

Chocolate-Almond Bagel Fondue

One 6-ounce package semisweet chocolate chips

2 teaspoons margarine

1/2 cup light cream or nonfat evaporated milk

1/4 teaspoon almond extract

4 bagels, cut into bite-size chunks

1. Place the chocolate chips and margarine in a saucepan, and begin melting over low heat.

2. As the chips start to melt, gradually add the cream or milk, stirring constantly.

3. When the chips have melted completely and the mixture is blended, add the almond extract and mix well.

4. Pour the warmed mixture into a fondue pot set over a low flame. Serve with bite-size bagel chunks and fondue forks for dipping.

Makes 4 servings

The Big Apple Bagel

Try this with a scoop of ice cream or nonfat frozen yogurt for an added treat.

5 cinnamon-raisin bagels

One 21-ounce can apple-pie filling

1 cup flour (all-purpose or whole-wheat graham flour)

1/4 cup soft margarine

2 tablespoons dark brown sugar

1/4 teaspoon ground cinnamon

1. Preheat the oven to 375°.

2. Slice a thin portion off the top of each bagel. (See art on pg. 82.) Using your fingers, scoop out the insides to make "shells." Freeze the scooped-out bits and tops for later use.

3. Place 1/2 cup of pie filling in each bagel shell.

4. Place the flour, margarine, brown sugar, and cinnamon in a small bowl, and mix with a fork. Then crumble with your fingers until thoroughly blended.

5. Spoon the crumb topping over the apple-filled bagels, pressing the crumbs onto the filling. Bake on a foil-covered cookie sheet for 30 minutes, or until topping is lightly browned. Serve warm. Try this with a scoop of ice cream or frozen yogurt for an added treat.

Makes 5 servings

Note: You can substitute 2 large apples for the apple-pie filling. Peel and thinly slice them. Place them in microwave-safe container. Add 1 teaspoon lemon juice, 1/4 teaspoon cinnamon, and 1/4 cup frozen apple juice concentrate. Cover and microwave until tender. Let stand to cool, and fill bagel shells with cooked apples, drained. Go on to step 4.

Bagel Rummy

Rum Sauce

1/4 cup soft margarine

3/4 cup dark brown sugar

1 tablespoon light corn syrup

1/4 cup light cream or nonfat evaporated milk

1/2 teaspoon rum extract

4 very fresh cinnamon-raisin bagels, cut in half horizontally

2 pints rum-raisin ice cream or use nonfat vanilla frozen yogurt mixed with
    1 teaspoon rum extract and raisins

1. Prepare the rum sauce: Melt the margarine over low heat. Stir in the brown sugar, corn syrup, and cream or milk, and bring to a boil. Remove from the heat, and stir in the rum extract.

2. Heat the bagel halves in the oven until warm.

3. Remove them from the oven, and immediately place a scoop of rum-raisin ice cream on each bagel half.

4. Drizzle with warm rum sauce.

Makes 8 servings

Coconutty Bagels

1/8 cup shredded sweetened coconut

1/8 cup chopped walnuts

1 teaspoon dark brown sugar

1 teaspoon soft margarine

1 bagel, halved

1. Preheat the oven to 400°.

2. Combine the coconut, chopped nuts, brown sugar, and margarine.

3. Spread on bagel halves. Bake on a foil-covered cookie sheet for 8 to 10 minutes, or until heated thoroughly. Cool for 5 minutes before serving.

Makes 2 halves

Cannoli Bagels

1 cup regular or part-skim ricotta cheese

1/4 teaspoon vanilla extract

1 tablespoon confectioners' sugar

1 tablespoon chopped citron (or the kind of mixed assorted chopped fruits
    used for fruitcake)

1/4 cup semisweet chocolate chips

1 cinnamon-raisin bagel, halved

1 tablespoon chopped pistachio nuts or chopped slivered almonds

1. Place the ricotta cheese in a blender or processor; blend for a few seconds, or until creamy.

2. With a spatula, scrape the cheese into a mixing bowl. Add the vanilla and sugar; mix well.

3. Chop the citron into small bits, and add to the cheese mixture, together with the chocolate chips. Blend well.

4. Place half of the mixture on each bagel half, and sprinkle with nuts.

Makes 2 servings

CHAPTER 11

Children's Favorites

Bagel bakers are glutens for punishment.

Buzz-Buzz Spread

1 1/2 tablespoons honey

1/4 cup margarine

1 heaping tablespoon golden raisins

Bagels, halved and toasted

Mix the honey and margarine. Add the raisins and mix again. Spread on toasted bagel halves.

Apple-Peanut Butter Bagels

2 bagels, halved
1/3 cup peanut butter, preferably all-natural
1/8 cup plus 1 tablespoon applesauce
1/8 cup finely chopped unpeeled red apple

1. Toast bagel halves.

2. Place the peanut butter and applesauce in a small bowl. Mix until smooth.

3. Stir in the chopped apple. Blend well.

4. Spread on the bagel halves.

Makes 4 halves

PBJ Bagels

You guessed it . . . an old standby in a new shape!

Bagels, halved
Peanut butter, preferably all-natural
Jelly or all-fruit preserves with no added sugar

Spread peanut butter and jelly on the bagel halves. Serve open-face or as a big bagel sandwich.

Oh-Oh French Toast

1 egg or 1/4 cup egg substitute

1 tablespoon milk

1/4 teaspoon vanilla extract

Dash ground cinnamon

1 teaspoon strawberry fruit syrup (all fruit, no added sugar)

1 bagel, halved

1. In a mixing bowl, combine the egg, milk, vanilla, cinnamon, and fruit syrup. Beat with a fork.

2. Pierce the tops of the bagel halves with a fork in several places, and place them in the egg mixture, cut-sides down. Soak for about 5 minutes; turn to coat both sides.

3. Heat a bit of canola oil or cooking spray in a frying pan; add the bagel halves. Cook slowly over medium heat until brown on both sides and cooked through. (The cut sides will need extra cooking time.)

4. Serve open-face. Top with blueberry or strawberry preserves or fruit syrup (all fruit, no added sugar).

Makes 2 halves

Circus Bagels

1 bagel, halved
4 tablespoons crunchy, all-natural peanut butter
1/2 banana, sliced
2 teaspoons coconut

Spread toasted or plain bagel halves with peanut butter. Top with banana slices and sprinkle with coconut.

Makes 2 halves

Pizza Bagels

1 bagel, halved
1/4 cup spaghetti sauce or pizza sauce
1/4 teaspoon oregano
1/2 cup shredded part-skim mozzarella cheese

1. Preheat the oven to 375°.

2. Spread 1/8 cup spaghetti sauce on each bagel half.

3. Sprinkle oregano over the sauce and top each half with 1/4 cup of mozzarella cheese.

4. Bake on a foil-covered cookie sheet for 8 to 10 minutes, or until the cheese bubbles and begins to brown.

Makes 2 halves

Note: If you like, add any of your favorite pizza toppings before baking.

Go-Fish Bagels

1 bagel, halved
1 teaspoon mayonnaise
2 fish sticks, cooked according to package directions
1 slice American cheese
Shredded lettuce (optional)

Spread the bagel halves lightly with mayonnaise. Place the fish sticks on one bagel half; add cheese. Top with shredded lettuce, if desired, and other bagel half.

Makes 2 halves

The Sugarplum Bagel

1/4 cup plum preserves
1/4 cup finely chopped almonds
1 bagel, halved

In a small bowl, mix the preserves with the almonds; spoon the mixture onto each bagel half.

Makes 2 halves

Note: For the cottage cheese lovers in your family, try spreading a thin layer on each bagel half, then top with preserve mixture.

Introducing the world's first four-ring circus

Soup Sponges

Heat up your children's favorite hearty soup, such as chicken noodle, split-pea, lentil, black bean, or vegetable. Serve with toasted bagels lightly spread with margarine. Dipping crusty bagels into thick hearty soup is a delicious way to enjoy them both!

Monkey Bagels

I tablespoon honey

I ripe banana, mashed

3/4 cup whipped cream cheese or cottage cheese

1/4 cup finely chopped pecans

Cinnamon-raisin bagels, halved

Mix the honey, banana, cream cheese or cottage cheese, and nuts until well blended. Use as a spread on bagel halves or as a dip for dunking.

Makes I cup of spread

Honey Dips

I bagel, halved and toasted

Margarine

Honey

Butter the toasted bagel halves. Serve with a small bowl of honey for dipping.

Circle Burgers

A child-size meat loaf that goes 'round and 'round.

I egg or ¹/4 cup egg substitute

¹/2 cup milk

³/4 cup uncooked oatmeal

¹/4 teaspoon salt

3 tablespoons regular or fruit-sweetened catsup (available at health food stores)

I pound lean ground beef, turkey, or chicken

4 bagels, halved

1. Preheat the oven to 375°.

2. Mix all of the ingredients except the bagels.

3. Spread the mixture on each bagel half, leaving a hole in the middle.

4. Bake for 40 minutes, or until cooked thoroughly.

Makes 8 servings

Grilled Cheese Bagel

I bagel, halved

I teaspoon margarine

Two I-ounce slices cheese

Spread each bagel half with margarine. Place a slice of cheese on each. Place in the toaster oven or under the broiler and cook until the cheese melts. Put two bagel halves together for an extra-cheesy sandwich.

Makes 2 halves

Pineapple-Cream Bagels

1/4 cup cream cheese or ricotta cheese

1 teaspoon dark brown sugar

1/8 cup finely chopped walnuts

1 pineapple ring, chopped, drained on paper towels

1 bagel, halved

2 whole pineapple rings, drained on paper towels

Combine the cream cheese, brown sugar, pecans, and chopped pineapple; mix thoroughly. Spread onto bagel halves, and top each with a whole pineapple ring.

Makes 2 halves

Florrie's Salad Bagel

A salad you can hold in your hand! Use any combination of salad ingredients the kids like. Adults can add some zip with thinly sliced onion, capers, and sliced black olives.

1 bagel, any flavor but sweet

1/4 cup lettuce

1 heaping tablespoon thinly sliced carrots

1 heaping tablespoon diced tomato

1 tablespoon salad dressing, your favorite kind

1 tablespoon croutons

1 teaspoon grated Parmesan cheese, if desired

1. Slice a thin portion off the top of the bagel. (See drawing on pg. 82.)
2. Using your fingers, scoop out the inside to make a "shell." Freeze the scooped out bits and tops for other uses (such as poultry stuffing).
3. Mix lettuce, carrots, and tomato with the salad dressing.
4. Spoon mixture into the bagel shell, sprinkle with Parmesan cheese, if desired, and top with croutons.

Makes 1 serving

Florrie's Fabulous Fruit Bagel

Sweet varieties of bagels, such as cinnamon-raisin, blueberry, and granola, are especially good in this recipe.

1 bagel, halved
1/4 cup cottage cheese
4 large strawberries, sliced
1 heaping teaspoon diced apple
1/2 kiwi fruit, sliced
1 heaping teaspoon diced cantaloupe

1. With your fingers, scoop out the insides of the bagel halves, leaving "shells."
2. Spoon 1/8 cup cottage cheese into each bagel half.
3. Decorate the cottage cheese with the fruit, starting with apple and cantaloupe. Finish with strawberry and kiwi slices.

Makes 2 servings

Bagel Faces

Kids love to create their own bagel personalities! Try this eatable artwork with a group.

1 bagel, halved

2 tablespoons cream cheese

To make facial features, start with these ideas or use your own:

> *Eyebrows: 2 thin green pepper slices or match-stick cut carrot*
>
> *Eyes: raisins, peanuts, grapes, banana slice*
>
> *Nose: carrot slice or grape*
>
> *Hair: shredded cheese, peanuts, or toasted "O" oat cereal*
>
> *Mouth: bagel hole itself*
>
> *Lipstick: thin red pepper slices carefully placed around hole*

1. Spread each bagel half with cream cheese. Don't cover the bagel hole; it's your bagel's mouth.

2. Place ingredients on work surface, and let the children add their imagination to create whatever they like.

Makes 2 servings

Cinnabagels

2 bagels, halved and toasted
2 teaspoons margarine
Cinnamon-sugar mixture (2 teaspoons sugar and 1 teaspoon ground cinnamon)

Spread the hot toasted bagel halves with margarine. Sprinkle with cinnamon-sugar mixture.

Makes 4 halves

Apple Butter Bagels

Bagels, halved and toasted
Margarine
Unsweetened, all-natural apple butter
Nonfat granola

Spread the hot toasted bagel halves with margarine. Top with generous spoonfuls of apple butter. Sprinkle with granola.

A Bagel Glossary

Bagel Chips: Very thin bagel slices that have been baked until they are crunchy-crisp; a bagel baker's solution for giving day-old bagels new life; use with dips, soups, or simply as is.

Bageled: To cut oneself while attempting to slice a bagel; e.g., Jack bageled himself this morning.

Bagelettes: Miniature bagels that are wonderful at parties, or for children at mealtime and snacktime; they also make great teething rings.

Bagel Flavors: Once available only plain, bagels now exist in a dizzying variety of flavors: onion, garlic, egg, poppy seed, sesame seed, coarse salt, pumpernickel, rye, cinnamon-raisin, wheat, honey-wheat, banana-nut, cheese, English muffin, cherry, raspberry, blueberry, chocolate chip, and, in California, even jalapeño.

Bagel Holes: There are none; unlike doughnut holes, bagels holes really are *holes*. There is no dough left over in the bagel shaping process, whether manual or automated. When bagels are made by hand, the dough is either formed into ropes and pressed together at the ends, or shaped into balls with the centers pushed through and widened with the fingers.

Bagelmania: A physiological condition that occurs when you're driving home in the car with a bag of hot bagels, fresh from the bakery; usually results in eating several before you get home. Side effects: telltale crumbs that stick to your coat or jacket, especially if you're wearing corduroy.

Bagel Maven: Someone who thinks he or she is an expert on bagels; frequently from New York or even New Jersey.

Bagel Purist: A traditionalist who feels that anything other than a plain bagel with a *shmear* of cream cheese is a fraud.

Black 'n' Whites: Bagels made with a combination of pumpernickel and plain doughs.

Cement Doughnut: Term of endearment used to describe bagels; considered acceptable if a bagel lover says it, heresy if it comes from anyone else.

Cheese Bagels: A thin-skinned whole bagel shell completely filled with a blend of blintze-like cheeses; a favorite of Canadians.

E. T. Bagels: Also called "Everything Bagels," they have many different toppings, typically sesame seeds, poppy seeds, onion, garlic, and coarse salt. A great combo!

Kettling: The stage in the bagel-making process in which the formed bagels are boiled just prior to being baked.

L. A. Bagels: Not a basketball term; bagels that are definitely mellower, with a lighter, less dense consistency, than their New York cousins; usually made with more yeast.

New York Bagels: Considered the nirvana of "bageldom" and the standard by which all other bagels should be judged, because the U.S. bagel industry had its roots in New York City; it is also believed that the excellent quality of New York water enhances both the flavor and crust of these bagels.

Shmear: A generous spread of cream cheese atop a bagel.

Special-Occasion Party Bagels: When it comes to holidays, you can buy green bagels for St. Patrick's Day, pink ones for Valentine's Day, and even red, white, and blue ones for Independence Day. For parties, order a 16-inch bagel from a bagel bakery and have it filled with lox, cream cheese, whitefish, tomatoes, cheese, or meats and coleslaw—whatever combo you desire. Slice it up and serve it to a crowd! Or order a 16-inch cinnamon-raisin bagel, write HAPPY BIRTHDAY in icing on the top, add candles, and you have the perfect "birthday cake" for any bagel lover.

Steaming: A mass-production high-tech process in which racks of bagels are rolled into upright steam-injected ovens; used as an alternative to the traditional method of boiling bagels prior to baking; results in a softer bagel.

Water Bagel: A term that actually describes all bagels, since all are boiled or steamed in water prior to baking; the boiling process is also referred to as "kettling."

Also of interest from the Globe Pequot Press

Beautiful Easy Gardens, First Edition $15.95
  Tips on Low-Maintenance Gardening and Recipies.

Enduring Harvests, First Edition $14.95
  Native American Foods and Festivals for Every Season.

The Sage Cottage Herb Garden Cookbook, Second Edition $14.95
  Celebrations, Recipies and Herb-Gardening Tips.

Gourmet Light, Second Edition $14.95
  Simple and Sophisticated Recipies for the Health-Conscious.

Canning and Preserving without Sugar, Third Edition $12.95
  A Book for Anyone Who Wants to Avoid Refined Sugar.

Substituting Ingredients, Second Edition $8.95
  Cross-Referenced Ingredients and Equivalent Measurements.

The Rice Cookbook, First Edition $11.95
  More than 80 Unique Rice Dishes from around the World.

Old Sturbridge Village Cookbook, Second Edition $12.95
  Authentic Early American Recipies for the Modern Kitchen.

The Boston Globe Cookbook, Third Edition $15.95
  A Collection of Classic New England Specialties.

The Edible Mushroom, Revised Edition $8.95
  Eighty-two Recipies and Tips for the Gourmet Cook.

The Martha's Vineyard Cookbook, Second Edition $14.95
  More than 250 Recipies from a Bountiful Island.

Available from you bookstore or directly from the publisher. For a free catalogue or to place an order, call toll-free 24 hours a day 1-800-243-0495 or write to The Globe Pequot Press, P.O. Box 833, Old Saybrook, Connecticut 06475-0833.